Fit to the Fifth

Diana Wandix
Lisa King
Jennifer Goode

P.A.H.G.S
Prosper And Have Good Success
www.pahgs.wordpress.com

Copyright © 2006

All rights reserved. No part of this document may be reproduced, distributed, or transmitted in any form or by any means, including photocopying, recording, or other electronic or mechanical methods, without the prior written permission of the authors, except in the case of brief quotations embodied in critical reviews and certain other noncommercial uses permitted by copyright law.

ISBN-13: 978-0615566184 (PAHGS)
ISBN-10: 0615566189

To those who encouraged, pushed, loved, waited, and sacrificed.
Thank you.

Do not be deceived: "Bad company ruins good morals."
1 Corinthians 15:33

PREFACE

FIT^5

Okay, Ladies. I'm not gonna waste your time with some grand intro, pontificating theory on how to find a good man, how not to find a bad man, or what true love really is. I knew exactly what I was looking for. I knew exactly what I wanted in a man, or at least I thought I did. When you're a nice looking, hardworking, God fearing woman like myself—and I'm only saying "nice looking" so that I won't seem conceited or full of myself, but if you want to know the truth, I could give a eunuch a rise, if you know what I mean—anyway, like I was saying—when you're a nice looking, hardworking, God fearing woman like myself, you want a man who reflects those same wonderful qualities. I have to admit, though, many times I failed to look at the whole package. I'd see one great thing and just assume that everything else was on point. You know what I mean. Like, looks to rival Terrance Howard, or so much money he could float Donald Trump a loan, or a faith in God so strong that it would make the pope question his own commitment to the Lord. Yes, they would have that one thing going on, but unfortunately, the rest of the parcel was still at the post office. Eventually, I figured out that I needed a man who was fit to the fifth. What does that mean? I wanted a man who was spiritually, physically, mentally, financially, and emotionally together. He had to be "fit" in all five areas to get my attention. Fit to the fifth. I wish I had figured that out sooner, rather than later. I could have saved myself a lot of trouble. But, I always say to myself, "Mia Gentry, when you've gone through the fire wearing gasoline drawers, you have a responsibility to help others to go around it." So, consider this a little self-help book. Get out your highlighter and notepad, because the story that follows just might help you find the quickest route to your fit man.

CHAPTER ONE

Spiritually Fit

Spiritually fit is first on my list. He has to have his soul in order. This is non-negotiable. I will NOT tolerate wasting precious time with someone I will not see in the hereafter. If he's right with God, he's right FOR me. Hallelujah! Where better to find a spiritually fit man than in church? We all know that men go to church looking for a good, God-fearing, extra fine woman that he can show off to his friends and take home to Momma. The word on the street is that all the good women go to church on Sunday even if they just left the club on Saturday. Why not apply that theory to men? So, I figured, since I'm in church on Sundays anyway—when in Rome, do as the Romans do; spend a little time after service chit chatting, copping a feel—I mean hugging, you know, checking out prospects on the usher board and in the choir stand. But like my Momma always said, "If you gonna do it, do it right." So straight to the top I went!

Pastor Morgan was the new pastor at Calvary Missionary Baptist Church. He was just a couple of years older than myself, easy on the eyes, had a really nice body, no baby mama drama, and since the church paid for the majority of his expenses, you know he had some money, right? But, the most important thing is that he was spiritual. As soon as our eyes met we struck up a friendly conversation that would very rapidly lead to an interesting relationship, to say the least. Once I set my sights on this spiritually fit man, I decided it was time to be more active in church. Hey, I always rise to the occasion. At our first meeting we spent a few hours in his office getting to know each other as new friends would do. He was raised in the church and came from a long line of pastors and ministry leaders. I was pleased to know that he was actually "called" to be a preacher and was not just a good orator who simply decided to major in theology. Somehow that made him even more appealing to me. We had lots in common. You might say that we were equally yoked. He was all the things that I am. He was athletic, outgoing, loved to laugh and enjoyed the finer things in life, *and* he loved the Lord. Heck! I found another me, but with a penis. Oh joy! What else could I ask for? Finally, I found my spiritually fit man, a pastor no less.

Not only did I not miss a Sunday after our first meeting, I didn't miss Bible study either. When Pastor Morgan spoke everyone listened. He was so wise and knowledgeable, and *very* personable. Every sermon and Bible study session gave me more hope. (Excuse me, Ladies! I'm talking about the Word now!) Pastor Morgan was a pillar in the community. He spent many hours visiting the sick and shut-ins and heading up revivals. Not to mention he had class. I liked that. A spiritually fit man who can dress nice and smell good does my soul well.

It seems I wasn't the only one feeling some vibes. One Sunday Pastor Morgan told me to meet him in his office after services, and you know I did. No one can ever say that Mia Gentry is disobedient. He told me he wanted to get to know me better outside of the church. The feeling was mutual. Of course we had to keep this on the down low because he had many admirers. But that was okay with me. As a matter of fact I kind of liked the secrecy of it all. Have you ever noticed how it seems like a single Pastor in the midst of a bunch of ticking biological clocks is like a colon with parasites? Okay, gross, but you get the picture.

Our first date was better than I could have imagined. I wasn't use to the chivalry thing. You know—opening doors, leading me by my waist, lending me his suit jacket, and pulling out my chair. I think the Temptations said it best: "Treat her like a lady." He must have listened to that song many times because he had it down to a *T*. Or, it could have just been all of that good church upbringing. Whoever got the credit…I was reaping the benefits.

We were so discreet that the play we went to see was in another city; one where we didn't have to worry about running into any of the church family; one where we could really let our hair down. As usual, he was the perfect gentleman. We laughed, held hands, talked, held hands some more. We dined at an upscale restaurant, De Fantaisie. (In case you didn't know, that's French for fancy restaurant). This was so much more up my alley than a movie and a Big Mac. He ordered the Boeuf Braise, after he ordered Coq Au Vin for me. Yes, yes he did. He was a class act (with *act* being the operative word…but we'll get to that later). Up to that point, he had me, hook, line and sinker. I was relishing the thought of finally having a romantic, sophisticated, fulfilling courtship leading up to the most beautiful love story. It was a much prettier picture than what had been my experiences with the "Hey baby, let's do dis thang" kind of relationships.

In the middle of our dinner, I had started daydreaming about being the Pastor's wife. I was lost in my thoughts when I suddenly realized he was sounding like Charlie Brown's teacher. Wah-wah-wah-wah-wah. When I snapped out of it he was saying something about the pressures of being a single pastor. I guess the dreamy look on my face clued him in to the fact that I was off in la-la land.

"Mia?"

"I'm sorry, Gerald." Oh, yes, we were on a first name basis. Sister Gentry and Pastor Morgan were formalities that we didn't have to front when we were alone. "I can imagine that it's hard being a single pastor, especially one like yourself. You'd be a great catch for any woman, and *every* woman in the church knows that." I looked down a little shyly as I said that. You know that coy flirtation always gets a man. Gerald was no exception. He reached over and touched my hand. When I looked up, our eyes locked like Billy Dee and Diana Ross's in *Mahogany*. Mia Morgan. Doesn't that sound good? Perfect, just perfect.

It wasn't until after dinner when I saw the first flaw. While we waited for the valet, he lit up the butt of a cigarette and smoked it like an asthmatic on an oxygen tank. "Gerald," I said. "You never said you smoke." He was so into that nicotine that he took two long drags before he could even answer me.

"Oh, yeah. It's my nasty little habit."

Nasty little habit? The way he was sucking on that butt it seemed more like an obsession. All the way home I couldn't stop wondering about what other surprises he had in store for me. My mind was telling me to get over it. Nobody is truly perfect. Everybody has some unattractive quality. Right? But, just last week he preached about our bodies being the temple of the Holy Spirit, and now here he is violating the temple. How could I be with a violator? I wondered how many Hail Mary's that would cost him in Catholicism. Oh, heck! It didn't matter. By the time he walked me to my door and planted the most seductive, soft kiss on my lips and whispered "Good Night" in my ear, I felt like I needed a cigarette myself—or maybe just a cold shower.

    I wanted so badly to share my excitement with my friend Carla. But, just as she answered the phone, I changed my mind. Carla couldn't keep a secret. Not to mention, the jealously would eat her alive. She had always envisioned herself as a pastor's wife and would absolutely hate the possibility of me living her dream. So, I saved it all up for Terry, my best male friend and fashion consultant, but, more importantly, my beautician. Two hours in a chair every Saturday—ya gotta have something to talk about. Not that I needed to find something to talk about with Terry. He was very easy to talk to. As soon as I walked into the shop that morning, Terry waved me over to his chair. I think we both looked forward to my appointments. Normally I would have commented on his tight shirt—it was sharp, but sometimes his fashion choices made me wonder if he were gay, or just liked showing off his solid frame—but today, I was so hyped about Gerald that I was about to explode. I gave Terry an earful.

    Gerald and I began talking on the phone every night. We became a little less cautious about our relationship, and three weeks later, we were spending time together in town, and during the day. I enjoyed seeing his competitive side when we played racquetball or tennis, but that was nothing compared to the night we played Gin Rummy with his brother.

One Monday, Gerald invited me over to meet his brother who was visiting from out of town. We had been going out for a few months but I had not yet seen the inside of his domain. That didn't really bother me. We had a strong sexual attraction to each other, and I just figured he didn't want to put either one of us in a situation that was too tempting to resist. You know what I'm saying? Anyway, I guess he thought that since his brother would be there, it would be okay.

Needless to say, when I got there, I was more interested in checking out his house than meeting his brother. I made sure I was looking super fine and adjusted my blouse before I knocked on the door. Just in case his brother answered the door, my boobs were not the first things I wanted him to see. The card game was already in progress. I chose not to join in, basically because I wouldn't be able to focus. I was too busy checking out the crib on the sly. It's really tough to be nosey when you don't feel free enough to get up and walk around. The most I could get away with was excusing myself to the bathroom and sneaking a peek down the hall. Next visit I planned on finding out just what was down there.

As I was coming out of the bathroom I heard someone ask, "What kind of shit is this?" Now, I didn't remember the TV being on before I left the room. Oh no! The TV was not on. It was Gerald!

"Don't pay him no mind. He hates to lose to me," his brother said.

"That's because your ass cheats," was Gerald's response. I sat down at the table and stared at Gerald in disbelief. How could my spiritually fit man talk like that? Those words just didn't seem to fit flowing out of his mouth. Flaw number 2. Okay. Maybe it was just a slip up. He is competitive, and he just got a little caught up in the moment—happens to everyone. The rest of the evening was pleasant. I enjoyed hearing their childhood stories over a plate of shrimp.

It was getting late and I knew Gerald had to get up early to drive his brother to the airport. We finally got a moment alone as he walked me to my car. "Thanks for inviting me over. I enjoyed the company, and the shrimp was really good," I said. Gerald said next time he'd cook me a full meal, so that I could see how good he is in the kitchen. To be honest, that wasn't the only room I wanted to see him work in. We made a date for Friday night. The goodnight kisses were beginning to last longer. If his brother had not been there who knows what would have happened. I pulled in a little tighter on the hug to see what I was missing. I said a very long prayer that night. I wondered if the penalty was stiffer when you commit fornication with a minister.

We didn't see or talk to each other on Tuesday. One of the church members passed away so I knew Gerald would be hard pressed for time. I couldn't wait to see him on Wednesday at Bible study. However, seeing him was not the main reason I went. My priorities were still intact. Sure enough, he was there looking just as fine and delicious as he always did. Now, I don't know if this was a sign or not, but he taught from Colossians 3:5-10. Correct me if I am wrong, but doesn't verse 8 say something about putting filthy communication out of your mouth? So strange that he would choose that particular scripture when less than 72 hours ago he was cursing at his brother over a card game. In my head I could hear Terry saying, "If it walks like a duck, and quacks like a duck, then it's a duck." In my ear, I heard Carla saying, "Isn't he fine? Call me tonight girl. I have something to tell you." I thought, "Yeah, right. That ain't gonna happen." Carla would talk you into a coma. After Bible study, I slipped out of the church without saying one word to Gerald. Questioning his integrity didn't feel good. A smoking and cursing pastor who preaches against both, was a little disturbing.

Gerald wanted to see me on Thursday. I told him I wasn't feeling well and that I wanted to rest. He offered to bring me some medicine but I declined the offer. Later that evening he called to check on me again. I let the answering machine pick up. "Hey, it's me. I was just calling to make sure you're okay and let you know I'm thinking about you. When you feel up to it, look outside your front door. Call me and let me know if we're still on for tomorrow." I felt bad for not picking up the phone, but I really was ill. Nevertheless, I dragged myself out of bed, opened my front door, and felt even worse. How could I have ignored such a wonderful man on Wednesday and refuse to talk to him on Thursday? Sitting in front of my door was the cutest Teddy Bear holding a dozen red roses and some Alka Seltzer Plus Cold Medicine. What flaws? Oh yes, we were definitely on for Friday.

The phone rang, again. This time I answered thinking it was Gerald calling back. Dang-it! It was Carla. I could tell she was really antsy about sharing something with me so I let her talk. She could never get straight to the point. She liked to paint a picture. Ugh! But wait a minute. Thank God for call waiting. When I clicked back over to Carla I told her it was a long distance call. Then, I clicked back over, told the telemarketer I wasn't interested and thanked him for calling.

Luckily, I only had a 24-hour flu. I was all ready for my Friday night date. Gerald was happy to see me and he was in rare form. For some reason he seemed a bit aggressive, but not in a bad, overbearing way. It was more of a sexy, "I'm fixin' to lay it down" kind of way. Gerald had those LL Cool J lips and that Morris Chestnut smile, and he walked like Denzel Washington coming at you in slow-mo. So when he grabbed my waist and planted a long, sensual kiss on me at the door, I didn't even pretend to mind. How could I resist?

Inside, the fireplace was burning, the table was set and the wine glasses were full. Dinner was great. I had never had a man wine me and dine me with a dinner prepared by his own hands. Gerald always said any man can get a good woman, but few know how to keep her. "I think I'm falling in love with you, Mia," he said. I didn't expect to hear those words that night but they were music to my ears. Dinner was over. It was time for dessert.

Later that evening, while we cuddled and talked, I told Gerald that he was full of surprises. He wanted to know what I meant, and while I didn't want to ruin the moment, I guess his little imperfections were still bothering me a bit.

"Well," I said. "You are much different one-on-one than you are at church. It's almost like I see the flip side of you when we're alone. Who would have ever thought that you smoke and curse? And now you just tied me up and rode me like I was Seabiscuit."

Gerald advised me that he is a man and he has needs. "I'm not perfect and I don't claim to be; and besides, you loved every minute of it." Okay—he got me on that one. How was I to know that the pastor was a super freak? It's funny how the smoking and cursing were harder for me to accept than the fornication. Now I'm thinking, even though I enjoyed it, that's flaw number 3 for him, number 1 for me. I reminded myself that I'm not the one standing in the pulpit on Sunday mornings. Somehow that still didn't make me feel better about it later. I'd been looking for a spiritually fit man, but am I a spiritually fit woman? I started to doubt myself. Oh, the hypocrisy of it all. Oh, well. I'll pray on it.

When I got home late Saturday morning my phone was ringing off the hook, and the red light on my machine was flashing "7" calls.

I picked up and it was Terry. "Did you forget your appointment this morning?" he asked.

For the first time in years, I had. What was the matter with me? I never missed a hair appointment, no matter what. Seeing Terry was like seeing a therapist and a masseuse at the same time. The way he listened to my problems and massaged my head…he was worth every penny. "Don't worry about it. I moved you to 2. Can you make it?" Terry was a godsend. He always had my back. Also, he knew I needed a perm.

I felt bad that Terry was disappointed in me when I told him the real reason I forgot about my appointment. I wasn't use to the silent treatment from him. Terry was a Christian and he knew the Word, so maybe he was offended by my actions. Shoot. But, if he was gay, like I thought, he had no room to talk. Still, I wanted him to talk to me like he usually did when I'd messed up, but he didn't. I needed to hear his opinion and his advice, but he offered neither. Oh well. He was pissed that I messed up his whole morning. But he said don't worry about it. Whatever. He'll get over it.

When I left Black Diamonds, that's the name of Terry's beauty salon, I headed directly to Carla's apartment. She had been trying to talk to me for days and 4 of those calls on my answering machine were from her. Since Terry didn't offer me any advice I thought, what the heck, I'll confide in motor mouth, if I can only get a word in. It didn't look like that was going to happen. Carla's mouth was running non-stop. Finally, I got an opening. Who knew she could run out of breath?

"Carla," I said. "I know you have not been trying to reach me for days just to tell me that you finally worked up the nerve to tell that jeri curl wearing, lazy, can't keep a job, 3 babies and a soon to be ex-wife having boyfriend of yours to get lost. You should have done that a long time ago."

Carla said she couldn't do that a "long time ago" because she didn't have any other prospects, and when he did work he would buy her some groceries. You heard me. She stayed with a loser for the sake of some meat and produce. I told Carla I had something much more pressing to talk about and that I really needed her advice, but first she had to promise not to tell anyone. She promised, but insisted on sharing her drama first. She just HAD to tell me what motivated her to let go of the loser. Here's what she said:

"You are the only one I can tell this to because I really don't want this to get out. Okay. You know I was helping out Pam in the church office, right? Well, before she went on vacation she was looking for this agenda that was faxed over so Pastor Morgan could decide what topic he wanted to speak on at the conference next month. Well, after she left, I found it, but Pastor Morgan wasn't there. So I went to put the information on his desk, but the door was locked. I know I probably should have slid it under the door, but I didn't. I brought it home. When I got home I got to thinking that he had been asking about it, so I decided to call the church and leave him a message. Girl, when I called the church, he answered. I told him to come by and get it on his way home. I never told you this, but I really like Pastor Morgan and I'd just been wishing I could kiss those sexy lips of his."

She laughed, so I laughed. However, my laughter was cut short when she said, "I got my wish."

"You what?" I almost spit out my Deja Blue.

"Yeah girl, I invited him in and we sat on the couch and talked a while and then I leaned over and kissed him, and he kissed me back. Then I did something else for him."

This was one picture Carla did not have to paint for me. I saw it very vividly introduced by the NBC peacock. So I stopped her. I let her know her secret was safe with me. I told her that if she really believed that there was a chance for her and Pastor Morgan then go for it. "He's available," I said. "But, if I were you, Carla, I would try to find a more spiritually fit man."

The puzzled look on her face told me that she didn't get it. That's okay. I didn't expect for her to. I left Carla's apartment feeling pretty foolish. What made me put this man on a pedestal? Was it my unrelenting quest to find what I considered to be a spiritual man? Who was I to define what makes a man spiritual? Does being spiritual mean being perfect? Maybe I was just totally confused. Yes, I think I was, but I wasn't a fool. What he did was wrong, and I planned to let him know just that. I went straight home and called Mr. Pastor Gerald Morgan. I wanted to go completely berserk. My plan was to verbally gut punch him. I wanted to ask him how he could tell me he loved me and then do something like this. I wanted to know if he truly believed in the things he preached about. But I never got the chance. I wondered if he had talked to Carla before I got to him, and she had mentioned that she shared their little sordid affair with me. Before I could even get out "this is Mia," he told me he had a confession. Do you know what he had the nerve to tell me? He said he struggled with lust. He's a sex addict! Boo-freakin-hoo! He told me all about him and Carla. He even said he felt bad about it immediately afterwards and asked for forgiveness, and now, he was asking for forgiveness from me. Can you believe it? Well, I forgave him, but things were never the same after that. I didn't trust him and I definitely couldn't tell any of my friends about us. Carla and I had a lot of mutual friends, and I didn't want her to ever know about Gerald and me. Call it embarrassment, guilt, shame—I don't know, but Pastor Morgan started to feel like *my* dirty little secret. Six months later I ended the relationship.

Anyway, I realized that I had a lot of work to do on myself. If I wanted a spiritually fit man, I had to be a spiritually fit woman. I wasn't completely sure what that meant; but I knew it didn't include smoking, cursing, and fornication. The bad thing was that I had to move my church membership. I couldn't keep listening to a hypocrite. So, I started going to the church Terry went to. Seeing him outside of the salon was kind of nice. Sometimes after church, we'd go have dinner or even catch a movie. In the beginning, Terry was just a Saturday morning confidant, but over the years we had become the best of friends. But I still hadn't worked up the nerve to ask him if he were gay. Why do women always assume that male hairdressers are gay anyway? Oh, well.

All the books on getting over a failed relationship tell you to find something to fill your time. So, I decided to join a gym. Working off some stress while getting physically fit was just what I needed. By the end of the second week, I was addicted. I was in the gym every evening after work, and early Saturday mornings before my hair appointment. Terry showed me how to pull my hair back in a cute, stylish pony tail while I worked out, and he hooked me up with an easy wrap style that I could do at home mid-week, since I was sweating so much. My philosophy is that even while you're working out, you have to be workin' it out. Right? Right. Well, my philosophy proved true one Thursday evening when I was just about to end my workout for the day. On my way out the door I felt someone looking at me. I turned around to see a cross between Taye Diggs and Mr. Clean. Hello!

CHAPTER TWO

Physically Fit

A physically fit man! Lord, Jesus, yes! Don't get me wrong. I have nothing against my "super-sized" brothers. In fact, I've had dreams about Levert—Lord rest his soul. But, let's be honest. Every woman would like for her man to be physically fit. Fat Albert may be able to hold his own, but chances are, you'll never know that, because at first glance, your eyes can't see it. Personally, I need visual stimulation. If a man is physically attractive to me, I may be interested in exploring the possibilities. My man—he has to look good to me. I'm talking, six pack, rock hard abs and thick thighs. Oh yes! Physically fit. That's what I want. That's what I need.

I was already addicted to the gym. I became obsessed. I had internal motivation, and now, I had some decadent external motivation. He was mocha; about 6ft tall and 235lbs of prime beef. I'm so glad I gave up my vegetarian ways. I love a bald headed man. I didn't talk to him the first time we checked each other out. I stopped at the vending machine and got a Poweraid, hoping he'd approach me, but he didn't. I didn't want to be too forward, so I just left. I knew I'd see him again. A hard body like that didn't come from only hitting the gym once or twice a month.

The next time I saw him, I stared so hard at him I could have burned a hole in the side of his head. He must have felt the heat because he suddenly turned, looked at me, winked an eye, and blew me a kiss. I caught it, put it in my pocket. "Did you give me that kiss or was it a loan?" That's what I asked him when I walked up behind him at the water fountain. Don't hate! He was feeling my flow. He told me his name was Vincent Cartwright. Cartwright? Wasn't that the last name of those Bonanza boys? You know, with the horses, saddles, whips and thangs. Hmmm.

We exchanged phone numbers and he promised to call. Honestly, I never expected to hear from him. Terry said that men would tell you anything they think you want to hear. But he didn't have to tell me that. I knew all too well. So, you can imagine how surprised I was when Vincent called 2 days later. I didn't want to sound too excited. I played it cool. I wanted to say, "What the heck were you doing that it took you 2 days to pick up the phone and call a sista? You almost missed out, because Mia Gentry is not a sit-by-the-phone-and-wait kind of woman. You better recognize!" (Shoot. Them fine ones get me every time.) But I couldn't go there. I'm too cool for that. I prefer eye-to-eye contact, especially with a fine man like Vincent; so, I suggested we meet at Grandma Kelly's Kountry Kitchen to continue our conversation. Who doesn't like good ole country cooking? Answer—Vincent.

Vincent very politely informed me that he did not eat flesh, and even if he did, he didn't eat after 6 P.M. It was 6:05. He admitted he was a health fanatic. My bad! I guess I should have known that. After all, he did say earlier that he worked out 5 days a week, ran 2 miles on the weekends, and started his mornings off with health supplements. Still, I took it as a brush off. Of course, that meant something was wrong with him, because surely there was nothing wrong with me.

"Why don't we meet tomorrow downtown at Café Azzurri around 3:30? They have a great salad bar."

Uh, oh! I was wrong! He does want to get together. But at 3:30 in the afternoon? I hope he has a J.O.B. "Sure. I'll see you then."

I made sure I was looking extra fly. I had on my Jimmy Choo Redford leather sandals, $610.00; and my Tadashi black strapless dress, $267.99. That's right, baby! Eight hundred seventy seven dollars and ninety-nine cents…Grand Diva. I had $200 in my $350.00 Prada handbag. Why? Because, I got it like that. Okay, okay, I also wanted him to recognize who he was dealing with, without actually bragging on myself. When you get a really fine man that knows he's fine, you cannot be intimidated. You must be very confident, so he knows you will NOT fight for the mirror. Ladies first.

Vincent was already seated when I arrived. I spied him across the room. There he was. A physically fit man, who could soon be mine, checking himself out in the spoon. When I got to the table he stood up and kissed me on the cheek. I thought that was sweet. He said,

"Wow! You look fantastic." I thought, "You're right, I do." Luckily, "Thank you" came out. Sometimes I can't control what comes out of my mouth.

Clearly Vincent hadn't eaten all day because as soon as my butt hit the seat he motioned for the waitress. "I'm starving," he said. "I covered for one of the other PT's at the gym this morning and didn't have time to eat." Okay. So now I know what he does for a living. He's a personal trainer. Which means he ain't got no money!

"Oh, you're a personal trainer?" I asked.

His response was, "Yeah. So now you know why I look so good." Now see, I probably would have thought something like that, but I never would have verbalized it. I did like the fact that he took good care of his body, though. And Vincent was breathtaking. He was conceited and extremely self-absorbed, but he had a great sense of humor. I'm a sucker for a man who can make me laugh.

When the waitress came Vincent took it upon himself to order us two glasses of distilled water with lemon. I wanted a diet Dr. Pepper. Vincent said, "Drink water. It'll clear up your skin." Clear up my skin?! Does he have cataracts? There's nothing wrong with my skin! Oops, I actually said all that out loud. Vincent apologized. He said all he meant was that drinking water would keep my skin healthy.

"And no. I don't have cataracts," he said. We both laughed. Then the waitress brought the water and we were ready to place our orders. I wanted a large plate of shrimp pasta. Pastor Morgan had gotten me hooked on shrimp. I also wanted to impress Vincent, so, instead, I ordered a medium field salad with basil-flavored olive oil.

"And you sir?" the waitress asked.

Now get this. Vincent said, "I'll have a large veggie pizza with everything on it; an order of fried tofu strips with ranch dressing; and a large basket of some of those deep-fried cinnamon chips with the brown sugar on them. Oh, and don't forget to bring some mustard dipping sauce, a soft pretzel and a side order of onion rings. And may I have another glass of distilled water, please?"

I couldn't believe it! This is the man who doesn't eat flesh, won't eat after 6, runs and works out just about every day, will only drink distilled water, calls himself a health fanatic, and yet he overeats. When the entrees came Vincent dove in. By the time I looked up from asking the Lord's blessing on my salad, Vincent was on his second piece of pizza, and all I said was, "Jesus wept."

"You ARE hungry," I said.

"I'm always hungry. I eat like this all the time. Just not after 6," he said.

I don't think he looked up at me again until he had eaten every bit of everything he ordered. I was in the middle of a sentence when he interrupted me abruptly and excused himself to the men's room.

Within a week, Vincent and I met at least 4 more times for dinner, just not after 6. We ate all the time! No movies, no dancing, no nothing! I noticed Vincent had a pattern. He always ordered no less than 3 entrees; he always ate everything on his plates; he took 'all you can eat' to another level; and, without fail, he would excuse himself to the men's room shortly after inhaling all that food. He wasn't binging and purging…was he? I hoped not. I wanted a *healthy,* physically fit man. Not one I'd have to nurse back to health because he pewks his guts out every day.

"Do men binge and purge?" I ran that question by Terry while he trimmed my ends. "Well, let's think. Has he ever asked you if his clothes make him look fat?" Now that was funny!

I invited Vincent to a private grand opening party for the spa addition to Black Diamonds. He agreed to escort me. I knew Carla would be there. Her family owned the barbeque joint that was catering the party. This would give me the opportunity to show off Vincent and my newly toned body. Carla would be alone, oh, and, she had gained a few pounds (smile). I stood back proudly and watched my handsome, physically fit man mingle with the crowd.

"That's Vincent?" Terry smirked. Terry was no stranger to the gym, so he was not impressed. But, it didn't matter, because I was.

"You better believe it," I said. "And stop staring because he's mine." Terry looked at me like I had two heads. But that's okay. Everybody knew Vincent was with me and I could feel the hate in the room. I loved it! I was feeling a little bad, though, that Vincent couldn't enjoy the barbeque. However, embarrassing as it was, he single handedly devoured 2 full plates of macaroni and cheese, 4 rolls, a bowl of baked beans (Yes! He asked for a bowl), 1 large salad, 6 deviled eggs, 2 pieces of sweet potato pie, and a slice of coconut crème cake a la mode and a partridge in a pear tree. I pretended not to notice. Sure enough, about 10 minutes later he headed towards the restroom.

Five seconds later, he returned with a forced smile on his face. I continued talking to beauty shop acquaintances and friends, keeping my arm in Vincent's all the while. I didn't realize that he was raring to go until he whispered in a perturbed kind of way, "Let's go."

"Sorry," I said. "I didn't know you were ready."

"I need to use the restroom, and that line is too long. It's ridiculous. It's just way too long. We need to leave. We need to leave now!"

Oh my God! Was he P.M.S-ing? He was freaking out like a roach at a light show. I'm so glad I was driving. I hated to think what could have happened if Vincent was behind the wheel. I could see the headlines now; MIA GENTRY KILLED IN CAR ACCIDENT, DATE SAYS ALL HE WANTED TO DO WAS PEWK.

Fortunately, I hit every green light. By the time we got to Vincent's apartment, he was cramping so badly that I literally had to help him up the stairs. He ran straight to the restroom. It was time for some intervention.

"Look, Vincent," I said. "I know what's going on here and it's disgusting. You have an eating disorder. It's called bulimia. It's NOT pretty, so stop it!"

Vincent was in denial. He said I didn't understand the pressures of having to look good 24/7. He said, "Look at me, Mia. Doesn't this outfit make me look fat? I've got love handles. My arms are getting flabby. I use to have a 12 pack and now I'm down to 6? My God, Mia, why is this happening to me?"

By this time he was practically screaming, but I listened. "You have the nerve to stand there and judge me? I'M A PT FOR CRYING OUT LOUD!"

That was the last time I saw Vincent Cartwright. I hope he is getting the help that he needs. On the outside he had the physically fit image I was looking for in a man. It's too bad that on the inside he wasn't fit at all. Looking back, I think my idea of wanting a man who looked good on the outside was a bit shallow. I mean, really. A person doesn't have to look like Mr. America to be physically fit. As long as he is healthy, I can go for that. But he has to be mentally healthy as well. I don't know what made Vincent see a distorted view of himself. But whatever it was, it was definitely all in his head. Note to self—next time, make sure the man you decide to date is not a poster child for the state mental institution. I didn't go back to the gym. Man, first church, then the gym. The next guy I date can't be a regular at any place I like to frequent.

A few months later I received a letter from Vincent. He thanked me for my somewhat tactful intervention and making him think about what he was doing to himself. I responded with a you-can-do-it encouragement card. I also received a wedding invitation. What?! Carla and Pastor Morgan! It was so sudden! Had he not grieved me at all? And she said those extra pounds were from all that barbequed beef she was eating. Yeah, right. It was beef all right, but it wasn't barbequed. One desperate hussy plus one horny Pastor equals one bun in the oven. Now, I want to pewk!

CHAPTER THREE

Mentally Fit

Well, needless to say, after the Vincent fiasco, I decided, once again, that I needed to take a break from men to focus on me. You know, that's really the code for, "Me and my man split and I don't have anybody else right now." I wanted to go to the movies with Terry, but he had plans. Huh. What plans did he have? I asked, but he told me it was none of my business. I have to admit my feelings were hurt. But, oh, well. I decided to have my own Black Movie Fest, so I ran to Blockbuster and rented all my favorites—Brown Sugar, Two Can Play That Game, Brothers, Best Man, and, just for a little throw-back, Lady Sings the Blues. All I had to do was imagine myself in place of the leading ladies, and I could have Taye Diggs, Morris Chestnut, Shemar Moore, and Billy Dee Williams. Perfect.

Before I settled in with my Afghan (blanket that is, I don't do dogs—at least not the four legged ones), popcorn, Sobe green tea, and tissue (for Lady Sings the Blues), I went in to do my evening ritual—shower, cleanse and moisturize my face, and wrap my hair. I kept the style, even though I quit the gym. It was easy and classy. Terry says he can always tell when I haven't been wrapping my hair, because my ends look frizzy.

While I was looking in the mirror I thought about something Star Jones said earlier on Larry King Live. She said that she always had this list of criteria that a man had to measure up to in order to be with her. Then one day, after she was morbidly obese (her words, not mine), she looked in the mirror and realized that she either had to change her list, or change herself. Well, I don't have that problem. I expect a lot from a man because I have a lot to offer. And that's not being conceited; I'm just keeping it real. I make good money in a job that I like, I own my own home, I don't have any kids, no skeletons in the closet, and I love the Lord. I just couldn't wait for Him to send me Mr. Right; and when you try to help the Lord, you just end up helping yourself to a mess. Anyway, once I got comfortable and situated, wouldn't you know it, the phone rang. Of course, I always think of everything, so I had my cordless lying on the arm of the couch; so, at least I didn't' have to get up.

"Hello."

"Hey, Mia! What's going on, girl?"

"Hey, Crystal. I'm just getting ready to watch some movies."

"Oh, is Vincent over there?"

I was not interested in telling Crystal all my business. Telephone, telegraph, telecrystal, if you get my drift. "No, girl. We're not seeing each other anymore."

"What? What happened?"

"Nothing, really. He just wasn't The One. What are you doing?" I had to change the subject quick.

"Girl, just studying. I'm trying to get certified to teach a couple more subjects. You know, the more you can teach, the better your job security. Teachers have to be very versatile these days."

"I hear you."

"Listen, I was really calling to ask a favor."

Here we go. "What's that?"

"Well, I'm getting ready to do a Black History study with my class, and you know out here where I teach MLK and Harriet Tubman are the only ones of us who are represented in the library."

"I can imagine." Crystal taught in a predominantly white school district way out in the boondocks. "Are there even any black students at your school?"

"A few, but we all need to know about the contributions African and Black Americans made to this country. Anyway, don't get me on my soapbox. There's this professor at Pellbrook College who teaches African American studies. I emailed him and he said he has some materials I can use. Since you're right there close to the college, I thought maybe you wouldn't mind picking up the stuff for me? Please?"

"Sure, I can get it, but then how will you get it. I'm not driving all the way out to your place. Sixty-three miles is too far with these gas prices."

"Don't you have an appointment with Terry this Saturday?"

"Yes."

"Well, I'll see him Tuesday. Just leave them there."

That's how the conversation went. Seems innocent enough, doesn't it? Well, nothing is ever what it appears to be. It turns out that Crystal had already heard that Vincent and I were through, thanks to big mouth Carla. Why is it that all of my friends are like worn out refrigerators? Cain't keep nothing? Anyway, it turns out that the "professor" was Crystal's cousin. Professor Damon O'Neill had seen my picture on her refrigerator and asked her to set us up. I didn't find all this out until the second date. Yes, we dated, but not at first. I was somewhat true to my period of self-discovery. For the first five weeks we just talked on the phone. I blamed work and a fear of getting involved again too soon, but he was patient and very mature about it all. I think that's what caught my interest. He was so intellectually and mentally mature. Drama free. Just what I needed—a mentally fit man.

During our month of getting to know each other over the phone, I found out that Professor O'Neill was all that and a bag of chips. This man had been a child prodigy. He finished high school when he was just 15. After that he went to college for several years and earned five degrees, yes, five! —a BA and MA in African American studies, a BA and MA in psychology, and a PhD in clinical psychology. I know that sounds unreal, but it's true. He was a genius. He'd been a practicing shrink now for 15 years. He said that listening to other people's problems for so long got to him, so he lightened his patient load and decided to teach a few classes in his other field of study. Wow! He was so smart. We could have a conversation about anything from the top news stories, to gossip about the stars, to everyday life issues. When I'd tell him about my girlfriends' drama, he was always the voice of reason and logic, giving me the perfect advice to give them. Just what the doctor ordered.

The first time we went out, it was wonderful. Damon invited me to the university to attend a forum on the effect of race on the diagnosis of schizophrenia. He said he liked to introduce these types of topics because it combined both of his fields of study. I didn't realize how much a smart man could turn you on just by saying something intelligent. The Today Show did a special just the other day, titled "Beauty and the Geek." It was about how a lot of beautiful women these days are going for the smart guys. Good thing Damon was smart and fine, because if he had been a Steve Urkel, I would have never given him my phone number in the first place. I'm just keeping it real.

Anyway, since Damon had to facilitate the event he had to be there early, so I agreed to meet him there. I wasn't quite sure what to wear to a college forum, so it took me a while to get ready. I finally decided on an A-line, faded black denim Anne Klein skirt and a black-cropped blazer, with black and white tank tops layered underneath. Damon was only a few inches taller than me, so I wore my silver, inch and a half heel Caparros sling back sandals. Subtly sexy and smart.

I decided to show up on time. We had already been talking for weeks, so there was no need to be fashionably late. Damon was the first thing I saw when I walked in the room. I had only seen him once before, when I went to pick up the information for Crystal. I thought he was nice looking then, but from this angle, he looked absolutely delicious. Maybe the outside looked so good now because I had already gotten to know him over the phone and really liked the inside. Anyway, he was standing across the room talking to a student. It was a side profile. Picture this: His hair looked freshly done. He wore it in a small afro and it was perfectly shaped and lined. I love a man with a freshly groomed crop. And whatever barbers spray on a brother's head after they cut it is like an aphrodisiac—I could almost smell it across the room. He was wearing a striking navy blue athletic cut suit that fit like it was custom made just for him. Of course, I hadn't seen him without a suit on, but I could tell that he was physically fit—not psycho bodybuilding fit, like Vincent—more like Pastor Creflo Dollar fit. (No disrespect, but Pastor Dollar can wear a suit like Oprah can work a weave.) That's all that I could see from the side—oh, his shoes were nice too—Bostonians, I think. You can tell a lot about a man by how well he takes care of his shoes, and Damon's said, "I've got it all together." He must have felt me staring at him, because he turned and looked right in my face. He flashed me the most gorgeous smile and I swear I saw light sparkle from those pearly whites, like in those Mentos commercials.

We met each other half way. He didn't undress me with his eyes, and he didn't have that "aw sukie sukie, now" swagger that country brothas do when they roll up on a sista', just before they smack their teeth and say, "Yo Baby, you be my Dairy Queen, I'll be your Burger King, you treat me right, and I'll do it your way, right away" or something along those lines. Ignorant. No, Damon didn't even try to cop a feel when he hugged me. He was the perfect gentleman. He gave me a friendly hug and rubbed my back like we were old friends. "It's so good to see you, Mia." He never stopped smiling. I was trying to maintain my composure, but that smile was about to make me melt like hot butter on a baked potato.

"Hey, Damon," I flashed *my* million dollar smile right back at him. "Great turn out." I looked around the room so I could stop staring at the man. I didn't want him to think I was desperate, or crazy, or something. When I turned back to face him, this time it was him staring me dead in my face. I kind of jumped.

"I'm sorry," he laughed, "I'd forgotten how beautiful you are."

"Well, that's not good. I always thought I was unforgettable."

"And you are. But physical beauty means nothing if there's nothing beneath that surface." He was quick. "Over the past few weeks, my attraction to the you inside has made the outside you even more stunning." Umm. Good save. And was he reading my mind. That's the same thing I was thinking about him. "Come with me." Damon led me by my waist. "I reserved a seat for you up front. When this is over, I'll meet you in the foyer. I'll have to shake a few hands, but I promise I'll be quick." I almost got offended that he wanted me to wait in the foyer instead of being at his side, but then I thought, "There you go, Mia. Don't rush things. You're not his woman, and these are his students and colleagues." I wouldn't introduce anyone to my circle on the first date either. Shoot, if that were the case, my co-workers' would have met enough men to rival the Million Man March by now.

When the forum was over I stepped out into the foyer to wait for Damon. I checked my watch, because I planned to give him 15 minutes. Anything more would be rude and inconsiderate on his part, and this time, I'm not going to ignore the *detour, dead end, and wrong turn* signs. At nine minutes, Damon was walking out the door. Impressive. "I hope I didn't keep you waiting too long, Mia."

"No. I'm fine. Are you sure you're finished?" You still have 6 minutes.

"I worked everything out earlier. Some of my students and one of my colleagues are going to wrap things up for me. I didn't want you to have to wait around for me." Pays attention to details. I like that.

Damon and I left the university and went to a twenty-five and over club called May Rain's Sanctuary (some women called it Mrs. because of the crowd it drew). It was owned by a jazz singer named May Rain who said she got tired of singing to "kids" who don't even know what real jazz is. So, she opened her own establishment and was very strict about the age requirement. The club drew a very nice, white-collar, mixed crowd. Women of all ethnicities went there looking for Mr. Right (and half of them went home with Mr. Alright, Mr. Right Now, or Mr. Down Right Wrong). As soon as Damon and I walked in the door, I saw at least ten women eyeing him. I needed to use the restroom, but I believe that if I had left his side those women would have swarmed him like flies on dog doo. So, instead, I slipped my arm in his and leaned in real close.

We found a table in a quiet corner and Damon made all the right moves. He pulled out my chair, bought me a chocolate martini, sat close, and acted as if I were the only other person in the room. For a while he just looked at me with what I would normally have thought of as a *stupid* grin on his face, but I was so into him that, instead, it was charming. He finally said, "So. Wow. I'm never speechless, but I'm just so excited to finally be out with you that I don't know what to say."

"Well, we could just pretend like we're on the phone."

"No, no. I want to be able to look at you, and touch you." Then he rubbed the back of his fingers across my cheek. Now, normally, that would not have been tolerable. Mia does not like for anyone to touch her face. But, tonight, I didn't mind. I was feeling good, and it had a lot to do with Damon.

At the club, we didn't do a lot of talking. We danced, and enjoyed the music and the food, but for the most part, we just looked at each other. I felt like I was in a corny love scene from a goofy love story; but I had been in enough nightmares lately that it was about time to flip the script.

We left the club around midnight and went to Damon's house. Now don't go gaspin'. I had no intention on hopping into bed with this man, and I let him know that before we ever hit the front door.

"Mia, I'm really not ready for this night to end, but I'd like a little more privacy. I want you all to myself. Would you feel comfortable coming to my home with me?"

"Look, Damon, getting to know you over the past few weeks has been great, and I've had a wonderful time tonight. And, yes, I'd love to go to your place and spend a little more quality time together. But before we even leave here, you need to know that this will be no Kobe Bryant case. I'm saying no *now*. I mean no. I do feel a tad bit tipsy, so if we get to your place and my body starts saying yes, the answer is still no. I do not consent to having sex with you tonight under any circumstances." Damon and I both started to laugh. "I'm laughing, but I'm serious."

"Yes, ma'am. I don't live far, just about five blocks away. Why don't we walk? It's a nice night and that will help knock the tip off of your tipsiness."

"That sounds good."

When we got outside Damon knelt down and slipped my sandals from my feet. "These are some bad shoes, but I know your feet must be tired from all the dancing. When we get to my place, I'll rub them for you."

Once again, normally, this would not be acceptable. I do not walk around in public places with my shoes off. But it was all so romantic, and my dogs were barkin'. I couldn't do anything but look at him and grin.

Damon's home was an elegant neoclassical Italian Renaissance style condominium. It was absolutely gorgeous. I could see myself living here. The ambiance was perfect. It had French antiques, renaissance paintings and sculptures, a marble foyer and very handsome hardwood floors. I could tell, though, that it needed a woman's touch to make it homier.

"You either don't spend a lot of time here, or you have a great housekeeper," or you're as anal as hell. "This is almost like a museum."

"You don't like it?" For a moment, that attractive, easy confidence that was so appealing in Damon disappeared. He looked like a child who had just shown his best friend a picture he had spent all afternoon creating, and the friend said it was butt ugly.

"No. No. I love it. It's exquisite."

"Thank you. Make yourself at home." Damon motioned for me to go into the living room. "Want anything to drink?"

"Water would be nice."

"On the rocks?"

"Yes, please, Sir."

"Coming right up madam." We laughed. How sweet.

"May I use your restroom?"

"Sure. It's down the hall and to your left. I know you just want to see what's down there, so go right ahead and look around. I'll give you the tour in a minute."

"Excuse me? Are you calling me nosey?"

"No, ma'am. I've just counseled enough women to know how you, generally, think. Not saying that you're like other women."

"Of course not." I headed down the hall and peeked in two other rooms before hitting the bathroom. Everything was immaculate. Just as I was going into the bathroom, Damon called down the hall, "Mia, I need to grab a few more water bottles from my garage to put on ice, in case you want more later. I'll be right back."

I took this opportunity to make a detour. I slipped into one of the rooms I had already passed by. It was his study. There were books everywhere—on bookshelves, on the floor, on his desk. But they were all neatly placed. Even the ones on the floor were stacked nicely in piles of six. I opened the side draw to his desk and you would have thought I just stepped up to a Walgreen's pharmacy window. Oh my God, he's a drug addict! Clozapine. Quetiapine. Risperidone. Haloperidol. I was about to slam the drawer shut and make my exit before he made it back from the garage, when I noticed one of the books on his desk, Diagnostic and Statistical Manual of Mental Disorders. Then I remembered that he had been a Psychiatrist for many years before he started teaching. Okay, Mia, calm down. These were probably samples that he often gave to his patients. I stepped out of the room just as I heard him coming through the door. I dashed across the hall into the bathroom. The medicine cabinets in there were practically bare. Only the usual band-aids, Neosporin, aspirin, and stuff like that.

When I opened the door, I heard Damon talking and he sounded agitated. "What are you saying? She said she likes it. I did my best and I don't need your negative input tonight! Leave me alone!"

If he were on the phone, I didn't want to disturb him, so I sat on the couch and started flipping through a coffee-table book titled *The Encyclopedia of the African and African American Experience*. When Damon came around the corner he looked startled.

"Are you okay, Damon?"

"Sure. I'm fine," his faced eased into that hypnotic smile. "Are you okay, Mia?"

"I'm great. I just heard you talking and you sounded upset."

"Talking?" Man, his facial expressions could change quicker than Brittany Spears could get an annulment.

"Yes. I thought you were on the phone."

"Oh, that. Yes, I was on the phone. Umm. One of my colleagues was concerned that our department head may have been, uhm, a little disappointed in the forum."

"Oh, I'm sorry, Damon. I thought it was great."

"Thanks. Listen, I don't want to talk about work. Let's talk about us." Now that, I could do. The rest of our evening was wonderful. We mostly talked. He was so intellectually stimulating. We also did a little cuddling and kissing—that was stimulating too. He walked me back to my car and I made it home around 5 A.M. I couldn't wait to tell somebody. I felt like a schoolgirl!

The first person I saw was Terry, that morning for my 8 A.M. appointment. I was exhausted, but Terry didn't seem to be too happy with me lately, so I didn't want to be late or cancel.

"You look like you've been out all night."

"Yes, and what a night it was."

"Who'd you sleep with this time?"

"Terry! I didn't sleep with anyone. Is that what you think of me?"

"Why would you care what I think of you?" Okay, now this was weird. Terry had been funny with me for over a month now, and I didn't know why. I know he didn't approve of the Pastor Morgan thing, and he was less than impressed with Vincent, but he was acting, almost, jealous.

"Well, I care a lot about what you think, Terry. You're my most trusted friend."

"Trusted friend, huh?"

"Yes. That's why I want to tell you about last night."

"You mean this morning."

"Whatever. Do you remember Crystal's cousin, the professor…?" I went on to tell Terry the whole story, even the part about the medication in the drawer and the odd phone conversation.

"Hm. You know, Mia, you have a habit of attracting the wrong men, or at least being attracted to the wrong ones. You better make sure that that medication wasn't his and that he wasn't talking to himself."

"What? Please. Don't try to rain on my parade because yours got cancelled." I was kind of mad at Terry, now. There was nothing wrong with Damon. I was sure of it.

As soon as I walked in the door, the phone rang. "Hello?"

"Hi, Mia. It's Damon." We decided to go on a picnic that afternoon and Damon insisted on making all the preparations. All I had to do was be ready when he came to pick me up. I wasn't ready. My mom called, and she likes to talk. So when Damon arrived, I was just getting dressed.

"Mia, didn't we agree on 3:00?"

"Yes, we did, but I got off track. I'll be ready in a minute, just have a seat. Would you like something to drink?"

"No, I'm fine." He sounded a little ticked. I know he's not trippin' over me being late. I hope he is not a punctuality freak. I believe in being on time, but sometimes things happen. If he's a clock-watcher, and anal about it…oh, we might have a problem.

When I came out of the bedroom, Damon was pacing back and forth. I stepped back in the room and peaked around the corner to watch what he was doing. This man was wringing his hands and…oh, no…it looked like he was talking to himself. Maybe Terry was right. I strained to hear what he was saying. It sounded like, "It's not good to be late. It's not good to be late. It's not good to be late."

I came out and shut the door noisily, deliberately, so that he would know I was coming.

"Damon, is everything okay?"

He jumped and quickly sat down, then jumped back up again. "Sure. Let's go."

"You're not upset that I was running behind, are you?"

"Well, it's just that when people are late, it can throw off everybody's schedule. One late person is like the first domino and his poor planning makes everyone else have to adjust and then by the time you get to the party, she's already started dancing with someone else."

"Huh?" Damon looked at me as if he were seeing me for the first time today.

"What?"

"What are you talking about, Damon?"

His face morphed again, and he gave me that smile, but his time all the gorgeous pearly whites in the world couldn't cover up the fact that something was wrong with this man. "I'm sorry, Baby. Being on time is one of my pet peeves. " He took my hand and kissed my cheek. "I didn't mean to snap at you."

You would think I would know better by now; but instead of cutting him off right then and there, I continued on with our plans. When we got in his car, he had two chilled bottles of Evian in the cup holders. He handed me one. "One for you, and one for me. Nice and cold, the way you like them."

"Thank you." I listened for the snap of the top when I opened it. I didn't want to wake up in a shed somewhere, tied to a bedpost.

Damon opened his water, and then took a medicine bottle from the glove compartment. It looked like one of the bottles I'd seen in his study. He popped two.

"What's that, Damon?"

"Oh, I have allergies, and since we're going to be outside, I thought I'd better take precaution." Allergies, my behind! Lord, just don't let him kill me.

When we got to the park, Damon spread a blanket on the ground and set up our picnic. "Damon. Why did you quit your psychiatry practice?"

"I told you. Hearing people's problems all day long just got to me after a while. Why? What did they tell you?"

"Uh. Who?"

"You know, Mia, you can't believe everything you hear. People say things because they get jealous of the work of others, especially if a black man is doing well. Oh, no. That becomes a problem. Yeah, I know."

Oh, snap! He's schizophrenic! "Damon, are you talking to me?"

"No!" He snapped at me like Lassie on a bone. Then, as quick as a flash, it was like he came to himself, "Yes. Of course I was talking to you. Who else is here?"

"Well, who is 'they'?"

"Huh?"

"Forget it, Damon. You know, I don't think this was such a good idea. I'm ready to go home." That's when Damon went straight Sybil on me.

"What? Why? We just got here. We haven't even eaten yet. I made sandwiches and cut up fruit. I knew she wouldn't like it. I said make chicken salad and buy crackers, didn't I?" He was talking so fast, I could barely get it all. "Be a psychiatrist, Damon. Be a professor, Damon. People don't understand the mental stress that comes along with success. And, Mia, look." He dug frantically through the basket and pulled out a little box. "I bought you a gift. We, I mean, I thought you were the one. See?" He opened up the box and it was a ring! "I was going to propose, right here under the sky. In front of the birds, and butterflies, and God. Will you? Will you marry me, Mia?"

This has got to be a joke. I had to look around to see if I was being punk'd, or was on that one show where people try to scare their friends. "Damon. We haven't even been going out that long. We don't know each other that well."

"I know you, Mia. How can you throw away everything we've built together? Don't you love me anymore?"

"Damon, I never said I loved you. I think you have me confused." I don't know if the medication kicked in or what, but all of a sudden, the smooth Damon I thought I knew was back, and his speech slowed down.

"I know it's sudden, Mia, and I completely understand your hesitation. I'm just a man who knows what he wants. But you're right. Let's get to know each other better first." I guess he could see the bewilderment in my eyes. "Are you okay, Mia?"

"No, Damon. I'm ready to go home."

"Are you not feeling well?"

"Yeah, that's it."

"Okay. Sure. I'll just save everything. We can picnic tomorrow afternoon, maybe after you get back from church." The whole way back to my house, Damon talked like nothing had happened. I was so disappointed. I really thought I had finally found the one. Damon called me for four days straight and left several messages saying how concerned he was about me. His final message said that he didn't know what happened, but that he could take a hint, and he hoped I'd find happiness. He really sounded sane but before he hung up the phone, I could have sworn I heard him call me a selfish bitch. I definitely planned to give Crystal an earful about her cousin. Surely she knew he was psycho before she hooked us up. Oh, well. Another one bites the dust. But what's the saying? *If it doesn't kill you, it will make you stronger*? I'm just glad he didn't kill me.

CHAPTER FOUR

Financially Fit

You would think that after such a mess of men I would be taking a serious hiatus from the dating scene, but on the contrary, I was more determined than ever to find Mr. Right. I thought surely there are some wonderful brothas out there who've got it together. Maybe I was just looking in the wrong places, and letting the wrong people hook me up.

I was thinking about my male dilemma as I was reading the newspaper. Neiman's was having a sale and a Marc Jacobs handbag caught my eye. That's when it clicked. Maybe I need to go for the gold. No sooner did that cross my mind; I noticed an article in the entertainment section of the newspaper that read, "Club owner, Eric Banks, is fast on his way to becoming one of the city's most successful businessmen with the opening of his third upscale dinner club, The Diaspora." I thought, mmmmmm…now, he sounds financially fit. I might have to go check the place out. After all, two of my girlfriends had been trying to get me to go to one of his places with them for several months. Ciara and Kenya were Wednesday night regulars, open mic night. Every Thursday morning before work, we would meet at the coffee shop where they would tell me all about the events of the prior evening. This was a cherished ritual, just like my Saturday mornings with Terry. Last night must have been live, because Ciara came into the shop talking loud and laughing. "Mia, oh my God, you should have been there last night. This bohemian looking white girl stepped up to the mic with a poem she called 'The Piano', talking about how she was in love with a married black man and how she would never give up on her man because black keys need the white keys to make beautiful music. Girl, she said, 'black must have white, coffee must have cream, hot chocolate must have marshmallows, Bailey's must have milk'. Then I yelled out, "You MUST be crazy!"

"No way, Ciara, you're kidding, right?"

"No girl, I'm not kidding. Anyway, then she pointed to him in the audience. The brotha started looking around, looking all embarrassed. The sharp cuts of the eyes he got from the sista's in the club could have sliced a brotha up. But here's the best part. Next thing you know, this petite black sista dressed in a business suit steps up to the mic and says, "I would like to recite a poem called, 'My little dick husband and his white whore.' There was no rhyme, mainly her comparing her husband's penis to everything small in the world. Girl, she even had one of her friends singing, 'It's a small world after all' in the background. After about 15 minutes, Eric Banks, the owner, had to just go and take the mic from the lady." Ciara was cracking up.

At that point I remembered the article and the accompanying picture of Banks. I asked, "Did you say Eric Banks? Do you know him?" Before I could get an answer Kenya arrived. Kenya said, "Ciara, I heard your mouth two blocks away. Did someone order my caramel macchiato? Ciara did you tell Mia about last night? That shit was funny."

"Yea. She was just telling me about it. What I want to know is if either of you have met Eric Banks?"

Ciara took a sip of her coffee, poked out her lips, swerved her head to the side and said, "Oh, hell, here we go again, what happened to Mr. Physically Fit?"

"No, no, no, girl. It was the nutcase last," Kenya whispered and elbowed Ciara while eyeing me.

"It's not important. Come on, give me the goods on Eric Banks." Ciara had only met him once at the club, but Kenya said she'd known him since grade school. Apparently they attended the same school up until his family moved to Dallas, Texas in the third grade. Kenya explained, "Eric loaned me a dollar in the first grade. When I didn't pay him back when I said I would, the jerk took my book bag and sold the contents. He made $10. I was furious. He's a loser. But if you want to meet the loser you'll have to wait in line behind all the other gold-diggers."

"Excuse me, I am not a gold-digger, I simply want a brotha that isn't living paycheck to paycheck. Way too many brotha's have no savings, no retirement plan, and no property, while I've been saving money ever since I got my first job at age 15."

Ciara interrupted, "Blah, Blah, Blah, Blah, Blah, we know you've been saving money since you were three years old but dang Mia, give the brotha's a break. Not all of them are as broke as a joke. You need to be tryin' to hook up with that tall glass of chocolate milk at your hair salon," she acted like she had to fan herself. "He is fine, and doesn't he own that shop?"

"Terry? Terry's my friend." I wanted to add that I thought he might be gay, but Terry really was my friend, so I didn't want to put him out there like that.

"Girl, please. Friends can do some things together. Um hmm."

"Whatever," I rolled my eyes at her. "Let's get back to Banks."

Looking annoyed, Kenya said, "Well, there is one sure way to meet Banks. If you can rhyme, you could try to win the poetry slam tonight. Banks personally congratulates the winner."

As I thought about what I could rhyme about, I heard Ciara say, "Oh my God, we've got five minutes to get to work." We simultaneously gulped down our coffees. Kenya said, "Meet at my house at 6:00 and I'll get us to The Diaspora by 6:30 so we can get a seat close to the stage."

At The Diaspora we sat close to the front of the stage, ordered some drinks and shrimp cocktail. The slam started at 8:00. At 7:45 Banks stepped on stage. He looked better than he did in the newspaper photograph. He was tall, somewhat thin, and clean-shaven. His salt and pepper hair made him look a bit older, yet distinguished. He was impeccably dressed, in a Hugo Boss suit.

He looked down at our table and we made eye contact. He gave me that look—the "I'm interested in you" look. I tried to be cool, but inside my head all I could hear was, "Oh yeah, he wants me. Of course he wants me, why wouldn't he."

Banks welcomed everyone to the club and then introduced the first poet. The first guy wasn't very good. But the relentless finger snapping of the audience for the second bard let me know I had to come with it. After several rum and diet cokes, I took the mic.

"I call this poem, 'My Mason Jar'.

> Sometimes I escape to a place I have never been,
> Not to avoid the reality I live in.
> In this place I see my world from afar.
> It's like seeing my life in a Mason jar.
> It's just a little tool of self-analysis.
> One I use sparingly, to avoid paralysis.
> My Mason jar tool. My Mason jar tool.
> I'm careful not to let it rule. Me.
> I haven't quite decided whether it's psychological or metaphysical.
> On that, I've got to think.
> But I can tell you without a doubt that it's cheaper than paying a shrink."

Dead silence followed. Then, Ciara stood up and with slurred speech yelled, "Now that's some deep shit, ya'll know ya'll need to snap for a mother f……..!" Suddenly, snaps and more snaps. More snaps than the good bard. Enough snaps to win the slam.

Shortly after, Eric Banks walked over to the table and introduced himself. He also brought over a pot of coffee. He said, "Congratulations, Ms…?"

"Mia," I replied.

"Well, Ms. Mia (smile). I usually just give the winner a free meal at the club, but would you be opposed to meeting me for lunch?"

"Well, that depends."

"On what?"

"My schedule."

"What about this Saturday?"

"I'll have to check my blackberry."

Having listened to the entire exchange, Kenya, the designated driver, had already written my number down on a napkin and handed it to him. "Saturday is good."

We agreed to meet for lunch at 1:00 at Casa de Pablos. As I looked over the menu, Banks asked, "So, what are you going to have?"

I said, "I'm thinking about the mushroom quesadilla's, what about you?"

He replied, "Great minds think alike." When the waiter came we both ordered the mushroom quesadillas.

The waiter asked, "Anything to drink?"

Banks looked at me and said, "Why don't we have some water?"

"Well, I was thinking more like having a margarita."

Eric leaned toward me and whispered, "Mia, you should still have plenty of liquor in your system from last night. Besides, the water will flush the toxins out of your system, and it is the middle of the day."

I thought, "Toxins, what's wrong with toxins? I like toxins. And it's the middle of a Saturday." But I acquiesced, "I'll have water with lemon."

No sooner did the waiter walk away then Banks excused himself to the restroom. Lunch was going well. When he returned, I asked him if the story Kenya had told me about him selling the contents of her book bag was true. He said it was true, but that he had made $30 dollars, not $10.

When the quesadillas arrived there was only one order. I said to the server, "We ordered two."

The waiter replied, "It looks like the order was changed to one."

I countered, "Well it must be a mistake."

Banks said, "Mia, the plate is huge, why don't we just share this one?"

"Well, I guess we could." No margarita, and only half my order of quesadillas? I was beginning to get annoyed.

Banks turned to the waiter and said, "We're all set."

The cost of lunch was cheap, $12.89. Eric said, "Including the tip, that will be $7.50 a piece." I was thinking, he can't be serious. So I rationalized. Maybe he has been out with one gold-digger too many and he was just testing me to get a reaction. Okay, I'll play along. After all, I do want a financially fit man. I put my $7.50 on the table. Eric said, "Well, that was tasty, but I sure didn't expect it to cost so much. Damn, I only have $2.50 on me. Mia, can you loan me five dollars?"

I hesitated. "Sure," I said, thinking this is definitely a test.

I would soon find out that it was not a test. Eric Banks screwed me out of $5.00, or so I thought. Somehow for the next three weeks, every time we went out to eat, he ended up making a profit and I ended up incurring a loss. Still, I thought this is crazy. He's financially fit. Could I be imagining things? No, I was certain Banks never paid for a meal. He always "needed to borrow just a couple of bucks" but never paid me back. I decided the next time dinner would take place at my house.

Dinner turned out great. Earlier that morning I had been sorting items to give to charity. I typically donated to Goodwill, Salvation Army, and my church. I have been blessed to have lots of material items, many of which I use once or never. The boxes included designer clothes, shoes, jewelry, CD's, DVD's, and a pair of workout pants that had "Mama Mia" written across the butt that a former male friend bought me as a joke. I was always too embarrassed to wear them out in public. Plus when the little blue flower between the Mama and the Mia that used to be visible was now lost in the crack of my expanding behind, I decided they needed to go. (Don't get it wrong. I could stand to put on a couple of pounds and still look good.)

Banks noticed the boxes in the hallway. "Hey Mia, what's in the boxes?"

"Oh, just some stuff for charity. I have so much stuff I don't even use. I hate to see it go to waste. You know, I have clothes in those boxes that I've had for years but never wore. They still have the tags on them."

"Mia, you have a lot of stuff here, why don't you sell this stuff, and make a profit?"

"No Eric, it's all for charity. I'm not interested in making a profit."

"What do you mean you're not interested in making a profit? That's the problem with most women, all they ever want to do is give their money away or throw their money away, and quite frankly their broke asses, can't afford to do either. You're never going to get out of this little apartment if you don't change your way of thinking and start making money."

"Look Banks, I don't need a lecture. First of all, this is not an apartment, it's a town home—a quite spacious one that I own, I might add. Second, I CAN afford to give to charity." Suddenly, I began to see floaters in my left eye, signifying an ominous migraine. I said, "I'm not feeling well, I need to go lay down."

Eric replied, "Mia, I'm sorry, I wasn't trying to upset you. Charity is a good thing. You are very giving. Let me drop the boxes off for you?" I told him I could do it later but he insisted, so I let him take the boxes to charity.

The following Wednesday the girls and I went to The Diaspora. I had not talked to Eric since he had left my town home on Saturday. When I saw him at the club, he was acting weird, like when someone knows you are in the room but tries to act like they haven't noticed you. Kenya and Ciara also picked up on Banks' strange behavior. "Mia, what the hell is wrong with your man? He's acting like he doesn't know you, like you're the invisible woman, like you're Casper the ghost, like …"

"OKAY KENYA! You've made your point, he's ignoring me."

Ciara added, "Mia, girl, what's going on? Are you and Mr. Financially Fit over?"

"No, I don't know what's going on. Maybe he's just really busy tonight." I couldn't believe I said that.

Kenya said, "OH PLEEEZE! ERIC, ERIC, YOOOOHOOOO, ERIC."

Eric couldn't ignore me now. He walked over to the table. "Hey Mia I'm glad to see you're feeling better, can I talk to you for a minute."

"Sure." I followed Eric to his back office.

"Mia, you know I really care about you but…."

I thought, Oh my God! No he isn't trying to dump me. Think fast Mia. You can't let him dump you first. I interrupted, "Banks, I care about you also, but I don't think our relationship is working out and I hope you agree."

"Yes, I agree. I'm just not interested in a relationship with someone who isn't just as motivated as I am about making money."

"Funny you should say that Banks, because I'm not interested in anyone who thinks that the only important thing in life *is* money, someone who thinks about others only in terms of potential opportunities for personal gain, someone too selfish to donate to charity, someone…well, you get the picture, and I really don't want to argue with you…so have a nice life."

"Goodbye Mia."

About a month later, Kenya, Ciara and I sat out on the patio of the coffee shop, when Kenya noticed a girl jogging in our direction. Kenya said, "Look at that skinny child trying to be all healthy and crap, I hate her."

"Kenya, you need to quit hating…it looks like Mia Davis, you know she has always been thin. Mia, don't you remember her? She used to work on the 5th floor of our building, we would call her Mia D so people didn't get you and her mixed up."

"Yea, I kind of remember her."

Kenya yelled, "Mia D! Mia D!" Slowing down just enough to say Hi, Mia D. quickly ran past us. As she ran past I couldn't take my eyes off of her. Ciara said, "Mia, why are you staring at Mia D's ass? Is there something you want to tell us?"

I jumped up and started running after Mia D. in my three and a half inch heels. "Mia D. WAIT, WAIT!" I yelled. By the time I caught up with her I was out the breath and my corns were throbbing. As Mia D. had ran past us at the coffee shop, I noticed that across the back of her jogging pants were the words "MAMA MIA" and with her flat butt, it was easy to see the blue flower between the MAMA and the MIA. She had on my pants! Does Mia D. shop at the Goodwill? I wondered. I had to know. I told her I really liked her pants and wondered where she had gotten them. She told me that she bought them on Ebay.

As soon as I got to my office I got on Ebay. Right there on the ultimate worldwide flea market were all my things. Banks was supposed to deliver my things to charity. I was furious. I tried for two weeks to get a hold of Banks. He wasn't even showing up at his own club anymore. Kenya told me her attorney boyfriend said I could take him to civil court. She added, "I told you he was a cheap-ass loser."

That Sunday there was an article in the paper, it read, "IRS allegedly investigating local businessman and owner of The Diaspora on failure to pay corporate income taxes on various business enterprises." It appears Mr. financially fit wasn't so financially fit after all.

CHAPTER FIVE

Emotionally Fit

Ok. Four more failed relationships…what's up with that? I took a long hard look at myself in the mirror. What I saw was a God-fearing, super-fine, intelligent, independent good woman, exactly what I always see. Any man's mother would say, "That Mia Gentry, now there's a good catch."

Terry was cheap therapy but I could tell he was getting burnt out on all of my drama. "Will you PLEASE flip the script? Either get to *happily ever after* or *The End*!" Dang! He acted like I had insulted his momma! The last thing you ever want to do is upset the person who's working on your head. I'm thinking, now is a good time to go visit the Women's Group Crystal has been inviting me to. Shoot. She should have been telling her cousin, Damon, about a therapy group. But, let me not digress. This needed to be about me. So, I took an extra-long lunch hour that day.

I went back at least 3 years and told them every torrid detail of my dating life up to date. I dated a lot of losers. Once I got my priorities in order and decided what I really wanted in a man, well, I thought I was on the upswing. Especially when I started dating the Pastor. But now, I think I was infatuated with Gerald, nothing more. With Vincent it was more of a lust thing. Damon had me all messed up. I really liked him. That was genuine attraction. Then, of course, there was Eric. I'm not even gonna' go there. But with so many failed relationships, I'm feeling kind of fragile. You know? I think I finally realized that what I really needed was a man in tune with his feminine side; a man who's not afraid to cry, someone who can use 'sensitivity' in a sentence but still be my rock. I deserve that. An emotionally fit man…that's what I really want. That's what I told the group. The group leader must have been related to Terry. She said, "Maybe you should attend more sessions. You seem to be a bit delusional. Are you on any medication that we should know about?" No she didn't! I only decided to share because I thought my experiences might help at least one of those crybabies to see that you really may have to kiss a few frogs before you find your prince. And, it's okay. Not all frogs give you warts. But, they just didn't get it! What in the world was I thinking about going to an 'Oh, woe is me' group session with some whinny, hopeless women? I don't know why I ever listened to Crystal. Okay, so I had a weak moment. I'm entitled to one.

I paid for the session but that would be my last. I was mad at myself for even sitting through all that blubbering. I filed my 'next session friendly reminder' in the parking garage trash as I walked to my car.

I wasn't feeling very pretty that day. On top of that, I was bloated and felt like I weighed 300 lbs. I couldn't wait to get home. Some hot chocolate, a piece of apple pie and a good movie sounded great to me, but for now, I had to figure out how to sneak back in to work without being noticed. No sooner did I sit down then Derek Dunn was calling my extension. Derek's office was two aisles over from mine. For months, he had been trying to convince me to go out with him. I told him more than once that I don't believe in mixing business with pleasure. The last thing I want is to be the 'talk' at the water cooler. I have too much class for that.

"Mia, when are you going to let me take you to lunch?" he asked.

"Well, not today, Derek. I just came from lunch. Maybe some other time."

"How about dinner?"

"No," I said.

"Let me come to your office and talk to you for a minute," he said.

I said, "I'm all talked out today, Derek. Plus, I'm not feeling that great." However, Derek didn't hear me because by then he was standing behind me. It was hard for me to be mean to Derek. Derek was about 8 years my junior. He was a really nice guy, easy going, his voice was very calming and he had the cutest dimples. If it was anybody else I would have said, "Look, what part of 'not today' don't you understand? The not or the today? Truth be told, if I didn't work with Derek I probably would have taken him up on his offer months ago.

"Mia. I know why you keep turning me down. You've told me a thousand times. You don't like to mix business with pleasure for reasons I totally understand. And, I'm cool with that. But things don't have to be complicated. All I'm asking for is a chance. Let me take you out to dinner one night. We can keep it on the down low. Nobody will know unless you tell. I'm willing to humble myself and be your secret lover, your boy toy…just use me and abuse me, whatever you want to do." By this time I was smiling and even laughed a little at his desperate attempt to swoon me. He was quite the charmer. How could I resist?

"Ok, Derek," I said "But, don't you dare breathe one word of it—else I'll be going to jail for homicide. And you know, orange is not my color."

"So, then I'll see you Friday night? Pick you up at 8?" he asked. All I could do was nod yes.

I was waiting outside when Derek arrived for our date. One—I didn't want him in my space, and two—I didn't want him to realize how much more money I was making then him. I had no idea where we were going. Derek just told me to dress comfortably. He insisted on it being a surprise. Surprise! "Go cart racing?"

"Oh, come on Mia, loosen up a bit, let your hair down. I promise you'll have fun," he said. Derek was right. That was the most fun I had had in, well, I don't know when. I didn't even mind that he took me out for pizza for dinner. (At least he paid for it. Banks would have charged me for every pepperoni I put in my mouth.) That night we sat and talked for 2 ½ hours. I asked him why a successful handsome man such as himself didn't already have a lady. He explained that he was once engaged but realized she wasn't the woman for him. He said she didn't understand him. He said most women are so use to being with men who treat them badly that they can't relate to someone who treats them like royalty. Who knew that Derek was so insightful? I kept thinking he is so emotionally fit, just what I want, an emotionally fit man. He was saying all the right things.

Derek and I became very close. He was easy to talk to. I felt like I could talk to him about anything and he would understand. We had managed to keep our relationship a secret at work. Actually, it was fun sneaking a kiss or two on the elevator. The possibility of getting caught was exciting. We began to spend lots of time together, even at my town home. Feelings were beginning to emerge. One night, we almost gave into those feelings, but I stopped him.

"Wait a minute, Derek," I said. "I do want you, but I really would like to take it slow. I've had some bad relationships in the past and I think it's because I didn't take my time. I don't want to make the same mistakes with you. It could get real ugly and eventually I'd have to cut ya." We laughed, but I was serious. I told Derek about my previous relationships, what happened, and what I would and would not tolerate and why. Derek seemed to be really feeling my pain. He said, "I understand, and I don't blame you one bit. I would imagine it's really hard being a woman. You put your heart out there and offer a man the best of you and all you get is drama. Men have to learn to appreciate a good woman and treat her like the queen she is. The men in your past, those men didn't deserve you, Mia. They just didn't deserve you."

It almost sounded like Derek was about to cry. I'm sure I saw a tear. He grabbed my head and held it to his chest. "Hmmm," I thought. "Was my story that pitiful?" I know I said I wanted someone in touch with his emotions, but I didn't mean it! I want a roughneck!

"Oh, sweetie, don't cry," he said.

(I'm saying to myself—"I'm not!)

"It'll be alright."

("I know!")

Okay. He's in touch with his feminine side. Most men have that "real men don't cry" attitude that can lead to an emotional breakdown from keeping things bottled up. Derek was sensitive. Emotionally fit. How romantical! He cares about me.

When I told Terry about it he said, "He don't care nothing about you! He's weak. A sissy." Terry said, "Brothers have enough hard luck stories of their own to cry about instead of crying over somebody else's." He went on to say that Derek was probably a predator preying on the emotions of unsuspecting women, just so he could get under their skirts. He made me regret that I ever told him anything about Derek. "Furthermore," Terry continued, "I don't think you even want him. You've been knowing him all this time, seeing him at work, day in and day out and now all of a sudden you just gotta have him. And, that's only because he acts like he's interested in your 'soap opera' life. You're just finally happy that someone accepted an invitation to your pity party." Pity party? Oh, I don't think so! Pity is not a word in Mia Gentry's vocabulary. Terry makes me sick! Despite his attempt to rain on my parade again, Derek and I were developing a meaningful relationship with lots of potential.

Derek and I went to a jazz club on Tuesday night. Since I live closer to work than he does and I knew we would get home late, I suggested he be prepared to spend the night at my place. This is normally not even an option, but I guess I was feeling good about Derek. I showed him to my guest bedroom and we called it a night.

In the morning, I was standing in the kitchen buttering my toast and I could hear Derek in the bathroom. The shower stopped a long time ago. I thought, "What is taking him so long? I like to get to work early. He is messing up my flow, but I am not leaving out without him. I'd have to give him my key, he'd make a copy, we'd break up, he'd start stalking me…yada yada yada."

As soon as I started to knock, Derek opened the bathroom door. Derek threw up his hands and screamed like a bad acting chick in a horror flick. I realized I was standing there with a knife in my hand. But for crying out loud, it was a butter knife, with butter on it! I busted out laughing. "Oh, my God!" he said. "Put that thing away, just put it away!" he said.

"Calm down Derek it's just a butter knife," is what I was saying but I was laughing so hard I really don't know what came out. Poor Derek broke out in a sweat, and he was shaking.

"Oh, so you think it's funny, Mia. I can't breathe. How's that for funny!" Ok, so Derek had an anxiety attack.

Later that day Derek saw me with some of our female co-workers whispering and laughing at the water cooler. He gave me the eye and I knew that meant meet him in my office. I had a door, he didn't. This is how the conversation went:

"I wanted to apologize for freaking out this morning, but I see you broke rule number one".

"Derek, what are you talking about?"

"You were talking about us, or rather, me at the water cooler, weren't you?"

"No, believe it or not there are other things in this office to talk about, you know."

"I don't believe you. I saw you look at me and laugh. You looked at me and then you laughed. You know…I would never bring our business to the office, Mia. We agreed to keep this relationship a secret, and just because I have a little anxiety attack, you thought you'd get your kicks at my expense. Well, it's not fair. I have feelings you know. So, if you don't want everybody in this office to know that you snore like a foghorn you'd better keep your mouth shut about me, Miss Gentry!"

"Derek, you are sounding very paranoid, and, might I add, quite childish right now. If you remember, it was my idea to keep us a secret, so why would I bring our personal business to the office?"

Derek stormed out and slammed my door. Now see, this is why I didn't want an office romance. Derek was acting like a girl. Not a woman, mind you, a girl. One of these days I will learn to be very careful of what I ask for. I started to think Derek is not emotionally fit at all. As a matter of fact, he is too emotional. How is he going to be my rock? I'd never seen a man throw a hissy fit before. The rest of the day we avoided each other like the plague. The more I thought about it, I knew I had to kick Derek to the curb, give him the shaft, drop him like a hot potato. When I got home that evening I picked up the phone to call him. But, before I could dial the number, there was a knock at my door. "That better not be Derek," I thought. It wasn't. It was the FTD florist. Derek had sent me some Tulips—my favorite flower. The note read, *'I'm sorry. Please forgive me.' xoxo, Derek.'* Twenty minutes later, I got another knock at the door. This time it was a balloon-o-gram; a dog in a doghouse with green balloons—my favorite color. I decided not to call him that night. I mean, I am not an insensitive witch. I surely couldn't break up with him after this, could I? No. I can't kick a brotha when he's down. I'll wait until Friday, that way he has 2 days to suck it up and get over it before he has to look at me again.

The next day was Thursday. When I saw Derek I could tell that he was dying for me to say something to him, so I did. I purposely spoke very business-like to him hoping he would get the picture and see that I no longer wanted a personal relationship with him. "Good morning, Mr. Dunn. Listen, I want to thank you for the flowers and the balloons. That was very thoughtful of you. I was wondering if we could get together after work for a few minutes. I have something I need to say to you and this is neither the place nor the time."

Derek said, "Sure. Why don't we meet at the Starbucks near your place around 5:30? There's something I would like to say to you as well." Ok. I got it. He wants to break up with me before I break up with him. How predictable!

When I arrived at Starbucks, Derek was already there, waiting for me, with a Mocha Latte—my favorite drink. On the drive over I had a thought. It probably was best to let Derek break up with me first. Then I could act like I'm disappointed, but inside I'd be jumping for joy. I could pull that off. I was named Ms. DQ (that's Drama Queen) in my high school yearbook. Yes. It would be better that way, especially since Derek was so emotional.

"Mia, let me get this out before you say anything. I know you think I'm a bit crazy at times but if I am, it's because of you. I have never felt this way about a woman before in my life. I don't know how to react to these feelings I have for you. Whatever I have to do to redeem myself I'm willing to do. You are all I think about from the time I get up until the time I lay down. I just can't get you out of my mind. You are the woman in my dreams. Give me a chance to be the man in yours."

Little did he know he was the man in my dreams—him and Freddy Kruger! Talk about a nightmare. If he didn't have those dimples, he wouldn't have gotten another chance.

Derek was on vacation the next week. This was good because it gave me time to see if I would miss seeing him at work. I didn't. Come to think about it, the only man I'd ever missed was Terry, and that's because a sista cannot be caught with her 'do' undone.

Derek called on Monday. He said he was going to Virginia later on in the week. His sister was getting married and he wanted me to help him pick out a wedding gift before he left. I agreed to help him. I love spending other people's money! I told Derek I would try to call him just before I left work so he would know I was on my way. Unfortunately, a late meeting kept me tied up that evening. I didn't get a chance to call, let alone go over. So, I called him on Tuesday. This time the conversation went something like this:

"Sorry, I didn't get a chance to call yesterday. Did you get the gift?"

"No, no I didn't get the gift, and what do you mean you didn't get a chance to call?"

"Well, I got real busy, you know 'needs of the business'."

"Oh, so busy that you couldn't pick up the phone for less than a minute to tell me you weren't going to be able to make it?"

"You're right. I probably should have made the time, but…"

"But, but nothing! Do you realize I sat around here all evening waiting for you to call? Oh, I guess you thought I had nothing better to do than to sit around here waiting for little Miss Mia!"

"Well, obviously you didn't, and where is all of this drama coming from?"

"I was really looking forward to us doing a little shopping, spending the evening together and just having some FUN! You know, this isn't the first time you said you'd call and then you didn't. What's wrong Mia? Uh, Ma Bell got her foot on your neck? Did you ever stop to think about how your un-thoughtfulness affects me? Oh! Oh, here's a better question. Do you ever think about anybody else's feelings other than your own? I had the whole evening planned and you blew it. You blew it big baby! And for what? Needs of the business! Bologna!"

"Ok. Derek, I'm going to let you go because you are obviously just a tad bit stressed out." He hung up in my face.

Derek never came back to work after his vacation. I think someone in the office said he transferred to Virginia. I thought, "Terry is going to love it when I tell him this." I'm so glad I didn't sleep with Derek. He'd want to cuddle and talk and all that crap. I don't know if I could have handled that with him. I sure feel sorry for the next woman he gets involved with. Derek Dunn was emotionally unstable, just the opposite of what I wanted. Maybe I'll try some reverse psychology. So I wrote in my journal…*the man of my dreams is a heathen, a big fat overweight one who is emotionally unstable, mentally challenged and broke as hell!*

CHAPTER SIX

Fitting It All Together

I decided not to share any of the Derek drama with Terry. He was really acting weird lately. My Saturday morning shop visits became less therapeutic and more nerve-racking. I use to be able to tell Terry everything, but now I felt like I was walking on pins and needles around him. I decided to ask him out for a Friday night movie. He said he had other plans, but then he called me later in the week and said he was free.

"Terry, I'm just gonna' be straight with you," we were sitting at the bar at the Studio Movie Theater, having an appetizer before the movie. "Something's happened between us and I don't know what it is. I use to love coming to Black Diamonds and telling you all my deep dark secrets, but now it's almost awkward. Whenever I tell you anything, you get upset with me, and for the past couple of months, you've been treating me like I stole something from you. What's up?"

"I've just had a lot on my mind, Mia."

"Well, share. I tell you everything. You can talk to me, too." Up until now, I guess our relationship had been pretty one sided. I was always in the chair and Terry was the friend and therapist. I guess it was my turn to be the friend.

"Just eat your calamari."

"No, Terry. Really. Is it a problem at the shop? Is your family okay? Did you have a fight with your boyfriend? What?"

This time Terry looked at me like I had *ten* heads. "My *boyfriend*?"

"Well, yeah." Terry looked angry at first, then he just smirked and shook his head. Then he got up, dropped some money on the bar for the tab, and walked out.

"Terry! Wait!" I got up and ran after him, and grabbed his arm at the door. "Where are you going?"

"I'm going home, Mia."

I stood at the door with my mouth open. I didn't understand. What did I say? By the time I got home, I had gone from confused to mad. How dare he leave me at the theatre and act so childish. I didn't know what was up with him, but I was no longer gonna' let him treat me like a redheaded stepchild. I didn't go to my appointment the next morning, or the Saturday after that. In fact, I didn't go to Black Diamonds for a month. I didn't even see Terry at church. I decided to start going to early morning service just to avoid him. Then Daylight Savings Time got me again. I forgot to spring forward and ended up at church halfway into Sunday school. I wasn't a regular at Sunday school, so when I walked in a class and sat at the back, I didn't realize that Terry was up front. The teacher was teaching from the 5th chapter of Galatians.

"'But before faith came, we were kept under the law, shut up unto the faith which should afterwards be revealed.' So, class, does that mean that now that we have faith, we don't have to obey the law?" That's when I saw him, or rather, first, I heard him.

"Well, until Jesus came, the Law had the mercy seat. Sacrifices could be made for sin and man could get forgiveness. But Christ was the ultimate sacrifice, so now no more blood sacrifices have to be made." I never realized how mesmerizing Terry's voice was. "Now, faith is what brings about our salvation, not the law. Yet, we will still follow the law if we love Christ, because he followed it when he walked the earth, and we're supposed to be trying to be like him."

I always knew that Terry was into the Word, but I guess I always thought it was somewhat hypocritical since he was gay. After class I waited outside the door for Terry. I didn't know what I was going to say, but I just wanted to talk to him. To my surprise, Terry walked out hand-in-hand, with a beautiful woman. She was hanging on him like a cheap coat. I was shocked.

"Hello, Mia. How are you? And close your mouth before you catch a fly."

"Oh. I'm sorry. Hey, Terry. How are you?"

"I'm great."

"Hi!" Cheap coat threw her hand out at me. "I'm Stephanie. You know my Terry?"

My Terry? "Uh, yes. He does…or, he use to do my hair."

"You need to tell whoever is doing it now to clip your ends," Terry ran a piece of my hair between his fingers.

"Well, I've just been doing it myself."

"I can tell." Oh, no he didn't! I know he wasn't trying to front me. "Why don't you come in sometime this week? I'll squeeze you in."

"Has someone taken my Saturday morning spot?

"Oh, that must be me!" Cheap coat. "My hair was a mess and I had an event, so I just took a chance and walked in on a Saturday morning. I heard it was almost impossible to get in Terry's chair, but you made it possible for me. Thank you so much, because I not only got my hair done, but I snagged this wonderful man." She squeezed his arm and smiled at him. Nauseating. "I couldn't believe no one had swooped him up."

"Yes, Terry's great." I still couldn't believe it.

"Yes, he is. But, hey, I'll be out of town this weekend, so, you take my spot. I'll let you borrow him back for one weekend."

Borrow him back! Honey you're in my seat, and you are on borrowed time. You've had your last Saturday morning in my spot. "Well, how nice of you."

"Yeah, that'll work," Terry nodded. "So, I'll see you Saturday. Try not to be late."

No he didn't! I was going to have some words for him on Saturday.

During church service, the Pastor announced a new member to the Board of Trustees. And who was it? It was none other than Terry Richmond. Well, well, well. Not only was Terry not gay, but he knew the Word even better than I thought he did, and he was more than just a pew warmer at church. Who knew that Terry was so spiritually fit? I had a lot of apologizing to do.

Instead of trying to say it all on Saturday, I wrote Terry a long letter and mailed it to him on Tuesday. When I went to my, yes, MY appointment, Terry didn't even mention my letter. Finally, I couldn't take it anymore.

"Did you get my letter?"

"Yes."

"Terry! How long are you going to make me suffer? I'm soooooooooooo sorry that I offended you. I just thought…"

"You just thought that because I'm a hairstylist, I must be gay. Well, not all male hairstylists are gay, Mia. And, yes, I'm offended that you thought that. No straight man wants to know that women think he's gay."

"I'm really sorry, Terry. Do you forgive me?"

Pause. "Definitely. You're my girl." Something about the way he said that made me feel all tingly inside. Terry truly was my dearest friend.

"Can I have my spot back, permanently?" I used my little girl voice for that request.

Terry laughed. "I can probably manage that. One of my other Saturday clients is moving to New Jersey. I'll give Stephanie her spot."

"So, are you sleeping with that girl?"

"That's really none of your business, but no. And you know how I feel about that. It's really, really hard sometimes—no pun intended—but I try to be celibate. Sex is meant for marriage."

I'll say it again: Who knew that Terry was such a spiritually fit man?

❦⋅❧⋅❦

It felt so good to have Terry's strong but gentle hands caressing my head, massaging my temples…so relaxing. It was great to be back in Terry's chair, my old familiar place. After a while I didn't even know what he was saying. I was enjoying watching his lips move though. I just laid back and gazed at him wondering what it was about him that had changed. Maybe he wasn't the one who changed at all. Maybe it was me. Something was different. I just couldn't put my finger on it.

"Well, do you want to go or not?" Terry asked.

"What? I couldn't hear you. What did you say?"

"I said I'm going to check out this new workout facility to see if I want to open up another spa. The owner likes what I've done with Black Diamonds and he's interested in doing business with me. Why don't you come check it out with me? I could use your critical eye."

"Is that the best compliment you can give me, Terry?" I asked.

"If that's what you want to call it."

That was the first time I ever thought that something was seriously wrong with me. To think, I actually missed Terry's sarcasm. Nevertheless, I said, "Sure why not. We haven't hung out together in a while. When do you want to go?"

"Come back around 2 and I'll drive. I'm interviewing some new stylists today and I should be done by then. Be prepared to work out."

When I arrived back at Black Diamonds, as usual, I was looking exceptionally fly in my brand new black silk spandex workout/lounging attire straight from the catwalk featuring the Sean John collection. Well, it wasn't really Sean John but it was something like that. Whatever it was, I rocked it.

As the owner took Terry and I on a tour of the new workout facility, The Fitness Challenge Center, I thought I heard a familiar voice in the café section, so I purposely lagged behind a bit. Sure enough, sitting at a table stuffing his face was none other than Vincent Cartwright, with his 3 entrees and distilled water. Thank God he didn't see me. I guess he didn't get the help he needed. Oh, well.

Terry was impressed with the facility and I was impressed when I overheard him say that he bench-presses 225lbs. After our tour of the facility Terry and I began our workout. This was the first time I'd worked out with him and let me tell ya, it was like boot camp. I hadn't planned on sweating too much mind you; I mean I just got my hair done. I felt Terry should have been sensitive to that fact, but I'm trying not to be self-centered. Terry floored me! On top of bench-pressing 225lbs, he does 30 minutes of cardio, running on the treadmill at high speed, and "the circuit." He works just about every muscle in his body! I knew Terry worked out, but I never knew he was so physically fit. I looked like a starving crack-head de-void of energy compared to Terry. It was pitiful, just pitiful. After 10 minutes on the treadmill I was done!

"Terry, I can't take anymore." I was gasping for air when I said that.

"What? What are you talking about? Stop playing. You use to work out all the time. You ought to be in good shape."

"Key word – "use" to. And besides, I was perpetrating. I came to be cute. I didn't come to work out this hard."

"Alright. Let's go. I need to get home anyway so I can shower and run an errand."

"Cool. What errand do you have to run?"

"None 'ya, as in none 'ya bidness."

"Well, I was thinking, I don't have anything to do tonight and maybe I can hang with you."

"You're kidding, right? You mean you don't have a man to sucker punch tonight? What's wrong with you? Are you losing your touch? You ain't hanging with me tonight. I have plans."

Terry hadn't changed at all. So I changed my mind and I just wanted him to shut up. I was only trying to play catch-up since we hadn't been on speaking terms for a while. He must not have missed me much. "Uhm."

Anyway, while Terry thanked the owner for his hospitality and talked about setting up a more formal meeting, I looked to the right just in time to see Vincent running to the men's room. I thanked God again, that he didn't see me.

Terry doesn't like to make snap decisions, so he told the owner he would consult his financial advisors and get back with him. And might I add, the owner, oh yeah, he was checking me out.

"Did you see him checking me out, Terry?"

"Probably because you have a hole in your pants and your left butt cheek is exposed."

Oh my God! I did! I did have a hole on the left butt cheek of my new Sean John …or whatever it was! I made Terry walk closely behind me so no one else would notice. He said something about going blind but I chose to ignore that comment. We had so much fun together. I guess I had almost forgotten.

※ ※ ※

That weekend seemed to come and go so quickly. But Terry was true to his word. Cheap coat, aka; Stephanie, wasn't too thrilled that Terry gave me my spot back permanently and moved her appointments. I guess she thought she had it like that…but…NOT! Yes! It's my world. She's just a squirrel trying to get a nut! Ok, now I'm aging myself.

Imagine my surprise when one day Stephanie showed up at Black Diamonds on my day at my time. "Stephanie. Hi. What brings you here this morning?" I asked just a wee bit sarcastically.

"Oh, I accidentally picked up Terry's cell phone when I left his place earlier this morning and I just wanted to return it as soon as possible. So, where is he?"

This trick was trying to be cute with me. She actually thinks that I'm competition for her. How flattering. And, that was a pretty slick move letting me know she spent the night with Terry. I wanted to burst her bubble so bad and say, "So! You didn't get none…not even a peek!" But, I'm a new woman and that's what I get for trying to be a smart-alec. So instead I said, "He stepped away to take a phone call. He'll be right back." I tried to finish reading the latest issue of Ebony, but Stephanie looked like she had something else to say. I was right. She leaned in closer and spoke just above a whisper. It was almost intimidating.

"Look Mia, I need to be honest with you. It bothers me that you and Terry spend so much time together. I know ya'll have known each other for a long time but Terry and I are trying to make something permanent out of our relationship and that's really hard to do when you're always in the picture."

"Well, I'm sorry Stephanie. I didn't realize I was taking up so much of his time. I mean, we've only been friends forever and that's what friends do, spend time together. But, if you have a problem with it then I can cut back on our hang-out time."

"Thank you."

"Sure. I mean…Terry and I are like brother and sister. You really don't need to feel threatened by me, Stephanie." Up to this point, I thought the conversation was going very well. But then, it took a drastic turn.

"Threatened? Did you say threatened?

"Yes. I believe I did."

"First of all, I don't feel threatened by you, MIA. I feel disgusted by you. You obviously have no life cause if ya did, ya wouldn't have time to be the 3rd wheel in Terry's and my relationship." Okay, I had a vision of bustin' her in the mouth like Vivica Fox did Gabrielle Union when she was trying to push up on Morris Chestnut in *Two Can Play That Game*. But just like with Vivica, it was just a daydream. When I snapped out of it, Stephanie was still in my face. "Every time the phone rings it's you, every time you need help with something you ask Terry, every time we try to spend a little quality time together, there you are like a little jack-in-the-box always popping up. So why don't you POP yourself right out of our space!?! You know, from what I've heard about you, you have no problems finding men, so I suggest you go find one and shower all of your attention on him."

Woo! Did this trick just try to read me?! "Had I known that you were so insecure, STEPHANIE, I would have turned down the times I was INVITED to participate in your little outings. It's not like it's a picnic being around you and your sappy sweet, sickening, syrupy whiney 'Oh Terry we were meant to be, this is fate, we're perfect together' bull crap! The ants have invaded camp, sister, and you are not the queen. Where the hell did you come from anyway? Now I see that all that sweet mess is just an act for Terry. You're a fake!"

"Fake! Listen! I am not going to stand here and trade insults with you. I came to you woman to woman to ask you nicely to back off, but since you want to be a bitch about it the gloves are coming off. You can sit there and say you and Terry are just friends, you and Terry are like brother and sister, and be in denial all the daylong. Just so you know, I'm on to you and this is one fight I don't intend to lose."

Keep in mind, we were still talking just above a whisper. I didn't want to make a scene in Terry's place of business, so I let Stephanie have the last word. I repeat. I <u>let</u> Stephanie have the last word. But, don't think I didn't hear her call me a Bitch while she was storming off into the wonderful world of Stephanie. She is so transparent. The nerve of her accusing me of sabotaging their relationship. She's so stupid. What reason would I have for doing that? That's what I asked Terry when I called him later that evening.

"Oh but we can talk about this later, Terry. She's probably on her way over and I would hate for her to walk in while you're on the phone with me. It might send her completely over the edge." That was funny to me so I laughed, but Terry didn't. All of a sudden he got real serious.

"It's okay. She called already. She's working late tonight. Besides I think you and I need to have a serious conversation for once in our lives. You know, you always have cards on the table but now it's time to show your hand."

"Okay. What are you talking about?"

"I've heard Stephanie's side of the story and now yours. One thing you both agree on is that you instigated the argument."

"What?"

"Yeah, you could have dropped it after she thanked you but you didn't. Why? Why did you feel it was necessary to feed into her insecurities? It's like you have an arterial motive. Are you trying to sabotage our relationship?"

"First of all, it was never my intent to feed into her insecurities. I don't have an arterial motive, and for the second time, NO! I am not trying to sabotage your relationship with her. All I did was, I, I told her the truth."

"And what is the truth Mia?"

"That I am no threat to her. You and I go way back, you know, you're like a brother. We're best friends."

"Well Stephanie thinks that deep down you want to be more than 'best friends' with me. She doesn't buy the brother-sister song and dance and I don't know that I do either anymore. We've been in each other's lives for so long and have experienced so many things together. We've always been each other's constant. So, I would understand it if your true feelings for me have changed. Have they?"

Silence is golden. Plus, I was so caught off-guard I couldn't find words, let alone form a sentence. So, Terry continued.

"For some reason I didn't think you'd be able to answer that question and I was right. Mia, listen. I'm being straight up with you so I want you to really hear what I'm saying. You come off like you're so confident, unshakable, and secure. But I know deep inside you hurt and you're lonely. That's the reason why you went on this quest to find your perfect man. Fit to the fifth. You want a good man and you deserve one. Nobody is perfect, not even you. I think you know that you've been focusing on the wrong men because you don't think you can have the right one. Show me your hand. Be honest with yourself and don't have any regrets. If there is anything you want to tell me, Mia, I'm listening."

What Terry said was so emotionally mature. It was like he was on another level; one that I couldn't reach. So, I did what I always do when I feel cornered. I went behind my wall and made light of the situation.

"Terry, I don't know what you want me to say. This sounds like a conversation I'm not ready to have with you 'cause I don't even know what you're talking about."
Silence.
"Okay. Okay, well I gotta go."
"You gotta go?"

"Yeah. I have some decisions to make, uh, about the spas and everything, so, uh, I'm a talk to you later."

Later for Terry was 2 weeks. He even had his assistant do my hair and he wasn't returning my calls. I didn't do anything to make him mad at me. Did I? No. I didn't. It was probably all Stephanie, The Great Interceptor's doing.

Was I falling for Terry? Was everything I'd been looking for standing right in front of me the whole time? Nah. He really was like a brother to me; a sexy brother, who I occasionally had incestual thoughts about, but a brother nonetheless. I blame society and movies like Black Shampoo. They always depict male hairdressers as gay. Maybe if I hadn't thought Terry was gay all those years, I would have noticed how much of a man he really is. Anyway, we've grown as brother and sister, not lovers. Get a grip, Mia.

※

"Hello."

"Hey, Mia, it's Terry."

"Well, hello!" and I wish he could see me rolling my neck. "Where have you been for two weeks? I know you're not dismissing our 7-year friendship because your 6-month girlfriend is insecure." Oops. I probably shouldn't have said that.

"Calm down. I've been busy with my business. Plus, like I said, I had some personal things to think through." Terry sounded a little distant. I didn't like that.

"Terry, I think we really need to talk."

"Actually, I gave you an opportunity to talk to me two weeks ago. That ship has sailed. But I do have something I'd like to show you."

I know he didn't. What makes him think he can dictate when and what we can talk about? Huh. He's not the boss of me. "Okay. What is it?"

"Well, I can't show you over the phone. Why don't you meet me at Johnny Carino's? I know you love their jalapeno tilapia...my treat."

"That would be great, except my car is in the shop."

"No problem. I'll swing by and get you."

When I hung up the phone I felt a little anxious about seeing Terry. What is wrong with me? I jumped in the shower, brushed my teeth, washed my face, and applied some fresh makeup, even though it was only 11:30 A.M. and I had done all that when I first got up this morning, and I hadn't been out of the house yet. This is too much trouble for Terry. I kept telling myself that, and yet I kept primping. I put on my BCBG Max Azria Herringbone print matte jersey dress. It fit me like a glove and accentuated all the positives.

When Terry knocked on the door, my heart started racing. Oh, come on now, Mia. This is ridiculous! I put one last dab of Donna Karan's Cashmere Mist behind my ear before I went to the door. "Hey, Stranger." I found myself flashing Terry that "go get 'em girl" smile I put on to impress a date. I had to laugh at myself as I literally shook my head to shake the smile off.

"What are you laughing at?" I loved Terry's smile. He laughed a little too—uncertain of what he was laughing about.

"Oh, nothing. I just tend to amuse myself sometimes."

"You need a dog or something. Laughing at your own jokes, told inside your head, is a sure sign of loneliness." Terry was being playful, but it kind of hurt my feelings. My expression must have clued him in. "You know I'm just messing with you." Terry gave me a kiss on the cheek. "You look pretty. Going somewhere after lunch?"

"Uh, yeah." I didn't want him to know that this was all for him, because it wasn't. I like to look good wherever I go. No matter who I'm with. That's my story, and I'm sticking to it.

We had only gone a few blocks when Terry's cell phone rang. Can she let the man breathe? For Pete's sake! I was so busy thinking nasty thoughts about Stephanie that I didn't even hear Terry's end of the conversation. I snapped out of it when he took a wrong turn and picked up speed. "Hey. Johnnie Carino's is that way."

"I know. I've got to take care of something. I hate to drag you into this, Mia, but I have a family emergency, and I don't have time to drop you anywhere. You're gonna have to come with me."

In all the time that I've known Terry, we've never talked in depth about his family. Was I that self-centered? Man. I've got to make some changes. "No problem, Terry. I don't know what the problem is, but you look like you might need some support anyway."

The rest of the ride was spent in silence. When I occasionally glanced over at Terry, I could see the tension in his face. I put my hand on his and asked if he were okay, but that seemed to make him even more uncomfortable, so I just put my hands in my lap and kept my mouth shut. That, however, was remedied when we pulled up at the State Hospital, also known as the local insane asylum. My mouth dropped open. Before Terry hopped out of the car, he hit my bottom jaw, "You're always tryin' to catch flies. Come on."

Terry met me at the front of the car and reached for my hand. I couldn't read his expression. "Terry, I'm confused. What are we doing here? Is this some kind of intervention? I'm not crazy, you know?" That's me, always making a joke of things when I'm uncomfortable.

"No." At least he smiled a little. "Can I explain later? I promise you'll be walking out the door with me when I leave." I smiled back and squeezed his hand.

When we walked in the door a woman who looked like Nurse Ratched from "One Flew Over the Cuckoo's Nest" rushed up to Terry. "I'm sorry we had to call you, Mr. Richmond. She was having lunch when she just went hysterical on us. She started fighting everybody and she keeps saying, 'Where's my son. I don't know you people. Where's my son.'"

"It's okay, Cathy. Where is she?"

"This way." We followed Nurse Ratched, I mean, Nurse Cathy, down a long corridor, and after a maze of twists and turns we ended up in a small cafeteria with blue-gray walls and tables bolted to the floor. There was a woman screaming and swinging her arms in a corner. She looked like a tanned Phyllis Dillard on crack. In a movie, it would have been a funny scene. She was wearing a pale pink dress with ruffles around the bottom and a yellow tulip embroidered on her chest. Three big, Charles Dutton looking brothas were standing about ten feet away from her with their arms crossed—just looking at her. One of them turned around when he heard the hurried footsteps of the nurse enter the room.

"Oh, Terry, how you doing, man?" He patted Terry on the back and they gave each other a "brotha hug".

Terry released my hand and headed towards the woman. "Momma." Momma? This was Terry's mother? "Momma. It's me. Terry." When she heard his voice, her swings slowed and she stared at Terry like she was unsure of who he was. Terry approached her slowly with his arms held out. "Momma, it's me." By the time he reached her, she fell, exhausted, in his arms and began to sob.

"My baby. My baby. Oh, Terry." Terry sat on the ground with his mother in his arms for several minutes. Then he picked her up and carried her to her room. One of the men, Nurse Cathy, and I followed. After he got her in her room, Nurse Cathy touched my arm and suggested that we go have some coffee cake and tea at her desk.

"I didn't know that Terry's mother was…was…"

"The politically correct term is mentally ill, Dear." Nurse Cathy smiled at me and patted my hand.

"Yes, mentally ill. How long has she been here?"

"Oh, I'm sorry, Dear. I can't give you any information about Ms. Richmond." She shook her head and pursed her lips real tight, as not to let anything pass between them. "Actually, dear, I'm surprised that Mr. Richmond brought you with him. He's never brought anyone here before, and he is very, very private about his mother's affairs." So, I changed the subject. I asked her if she knew Professor/Dr Damon O'Neill. I was trying to amuse myself but she said, "Yes. But he won't be having visitors for quite a while." You could have bought me for a dime. That dern Crystal! I KNOW she knew that fool was crazy!!

Cathy (she asked me to drop the nurse part), and I sat and talked a whole lot about nothing for about an hour before Terry finally came back to the front desk. "I'm sorry, Mia. I didn't mean to leave you out here by yourself for so long."

"She wasn't by herself," Cathy chimed in. "We've had a lovely chat. Haven't we, dear?"

"We sure have." I lied. Terry could tell that my smile was fake and he laughed. I was glad to see him a little less tense."

"You bring her back now, Mr. Richmond. It's good to have somebody to share the good and the bad with."

"Yes, Ma'am." Terry gave Cathy a hug, and we walked out the door.

As soon as we got in the car, Terry began to tell me about his mother. Apparently, she suffered from extreme postpartum depression after having each of her five children. Terry was the oldest—twelve years older than the youngest. When the last child was 13 months, she pulled an Andrea Yeats and drowned her. Terry said she would have harmed the rest of them, but he managed to hide the others in a closet and call his father. Terry said that after that, his father had her committed and never spoke to her again. He never took the kids to see her, but once a month, Terry would skip school, ride his bike to the train station, and take two trains to see his mother. Heavy.

"I'm sorry, Terry. Do your brother and your sisters go see her now?"

"No. They'd rather not."

"You've been dealing with this all by yourself, all these years. Wow. That's a trip. That has to be so burdensome." Terry looked at me like I had just said Nia Long is ugly (he thinks she's fine…huh…she ain't all that). "What did I say?"

"Mia, sometimes—I tell you—you're just so unbelievably selfish. She's not a burden. She's my mother. Depression can happen to anybody, and after a woman has a child her hormones can be all out of whack and contribute to severe depression or even psychosis, like in my mother's case. Had she been in her right mind, she would never have hurt any of us. After she got the right treatment and really realized what she had done to her own child, she just lost it. She refused her medicine. She tried to commit suicide. She's sick, but she's still my mother."

Needless to say, I felt about 2 inches tall. Even though his momma was crazy, I mean, mentally ill, Terry was definitely mentally fit. I rode the rest of the way home slouched in my seat like a child who was just reprimanded. Yes, I said home. We didn't even go to Johnny Carino's. Terry just dropped me off and said he'd talk to me later. Shoot.

The next day I emailed Terry from work. *Hey buddy ole pal, just wanted to check on you, make sure you're okay. I know you were real concerned about your Mother yesterday. You know they say the fruit doesn't fall far from the tree! I'm only kidding. I figure you'll either laugh because I'm so stupid or be angry because I'm so stupid. Either way, at least I've accomplished my goal of taking your mind off of it. Seriously, I'm certain better days are ahead.*

Call me if you need anything, anything at all. And, don't think I've forgotten about Johnny Carino's. I'm anxious to see what you wanted to show me.

Surprisingly enough, Terry responded exactly 10 minutes later. *Mia, thanks for checking on me, but it's all good. Yesterday was only new for you...I'm used to it. And yes, you are stupid, but in a good way. Johnny Carino's? I know you haven't forgotten about a free meal. That's probably why you were busting out of your pants at the workout center that day. Ha! Anyway, I do have something very important I want to show you. But, I'm real busy today and I am going out of town tomorrow. I won't be back until next Tuesday so I'll either cancel your hair appointment for Saturday or you can keep it and let Felecia hook you up. Call the salon and let her know what you want to do. I've got to go now but I'll call you later on in the week. Peace.*

That was on Monday, a week and a day before Terry's return. Things had changed between Terry and I; or so I thought they had. I kept thinking about the conversation we had the day Stephanie and I got into it. The more I thought about it the more I felt like I missed something. I felt like I missed...wait a minute. That's it. I missed it. Terry gave me a chance and I missed it. Wow. All of a sudden I totally got what he was saying.

⊱⋅⋅⋅

While Terry was away I took that time to do some real soul searching. I wanted to call Crystal and bounce some thoughts off of her, but then I thought, no. She thinks her cousin is sane. How can she give me good advice? I bet her whole family is whacko! Then there was Ciara and Kenya. I almost picked up the phone but then I remembered. Ghetto is as ghetto does! No way! Ciara would have me on Jerry Springer. That's where she got all of her advice. Oprah was Kenya's therapist. I could hear Kenya saying, "When you know better you do better." That's the last thing I wanted to hear from someone who doesn't have a clue and knows absolutely nothing about relationships. I didn't even want to think about Carla. Terry was the one I confided in and the one who would give me the best advice. But this was about him. There's no way I could even pretend like it wasn't. He would see right through the old *I have a friend who has a problem* line. He knew me too well. Sometimes I wished I didn't live so far away from family. I guess I could have called home. But then I'd have to go back to day one and try to explain the dilemma…too much drama. Plus, Mom would want to know when I was going to get married and give her some grandbabies. Dad would grill me about why I didn't take a job closer to home. I love them but I just didn't feel like explaining or defending my actions to them, not right now. So instead, I turned off all the lights and the TV, sat myself in my big bay window and watched the rainfall. I wondered what Terry was doing and if Stephanie was with him. That thought really bothered me. Somehow the sound of the rain falling and the thunder helped me to think better. I think it was at that moment that I realized that I had been lying to myself for so long. Truth is, I stopped thinking of Terry as a brother or just a best-friend months ago, maybe years. I had been in such denial I couldn't even remember when my feelings changed. I'd loved him for so long. Did

I say love? Yes. I finally admitted it to myself. Gerald, Vincent, Derek, Damon, Eric…they were just band-aids that I was willing to use to cover up my insecurities. Admitting that I had insecurities was a big step for me. I hid behind all of the expensive clothes and high dollar material things. I guess I did that because deep down inside I didn't truly believe that I was good enough for someone like Terry. I know that's why I tried to make myself believe he was gay. Here I was looking for a man fit to the 5th when inside I felt like a –4.5 myself. Part of me thinks I went through all of those relationships just to have something to talk to Terry about on Saturdays. As if I thought in some twisted way it would keep him interested in me, or make him jealous, or maybe I was afraid that if it had not been for my drama we wouldn't have much to talk about. I should have just been me. I wondered when and why I had changed. It hadn't always been that way. Silly me. I already know the answer to my questions. Things changed when I realized that Terry was that fit to the fifth man that I had been searching for, but I was too afraid to take a chance. I did want a man fit to the fifth but once I realized it was Terry I was intimidated. I mean, he's a Christian man, in good shape, intellectually stimulating, a successful entrepreneur and the most stable man I know. Just what I dreamed of; a man spiritually, physically, mentally, financially, and emotionally fit. What was I supposed to do? I didn't want to ruin a good friendship. But now I'm thinking, all the really good relationships start out with a solid friendship anyway. So, I made up my mind. I told myself over and over again, when Terry gets back in town I am going to tell him I'm in love with him and I want him, and not just as a friend, definitely not a brother. I felt good about that decision. I couldn't stop smiling.

✥

Thursday morning before work Ciara, Kenya and I met at the coffee shop like we always did. "Good morning, ladies. Sorry I'm late. I've been sleeping so good these past few days. Ya'll get whatever you want it's on me." That's how good I was feeling.

"Uhn uhn, hold up. You ain't never offered to pay when it wasn't your turn. What's up with that?"

"See, Ciara. You should really stop watching so much Jerry Springer. It's making you suspicious of everything." And, I wasn't exaggerating. Ciara is suspicious of everything. One day in a team meeting at work, our director said something about going over group expenses, and somehow Ciara got it in her head that what he was really saying is that he was going to be checking everyone's company credit card and if he found some illegitimate charges, people will be fired. All of a sudden Ciara stormed out of the meeting and started packing up her personal belongings. Of course, I excused myself and went after her. She said, "Ain't nobody gonna be threatening me with my job just because I dress better than anybody in here and I don't appreciate him accusing me of shopping with the company credit card. Just because mine was denied don't mean I'm stealing from this company. I ain't got to steal from nobody. I takes care of my own. He done pissed me off. He don't know me…we ain't cool like that, putting my business up for grabs. I don't need this job, hell, I was looking for one when I found this one." That's exactly what she said. How she manages to keep her job is a mystery to me.

"Yeah, Mia, what is up with that? Kenya had to put her two cents in. "You are awfully cheery this morning. Did we get some last night or what?"

"I don't know what 'we' got last night but I spent the night by myself, and I'm just happy, that's all. Dang, a sista can't be happy without something being 'up' or what? I mean, I can just pay for my own coffee and kill all of that noise right now." I knew that would shut them up, and it did.

☙❧

I looked for Terry to call that evening but he didn't. He didn't say what day he would call but I guess I was just ready to finally open up to him; show him my hand as he so eloquently put it. My nervousness had turned to excitement. Friday I didn't go straight home after work. I can't believe I volunteered to give a co-worker a ride home, 2 miles in the opposite direction. I could tell by the look on her face that she couldn't believe it either. I wonder if they all thought I was a conceited snob. I'd heard rumors but I didn't believe them. When I got home I had 3 calls on my answering machine. I was hoping Terry would call me on my cell phone, that way I'd be sure to get his call wherever I was. The first call was from a telemarketer. Seems someone turned my name into Jenny Craig, a nasty little dig from Stephanie I'm sure. The second call was Carla. What a surprise. This was her message: *Hey Mia, it's Carla. We haven't talked in a while so I thought I'd call just to say hi, I hope all is well. Sorry for not keeping in touch but I've been so busy. In case you haven't heard Gerald and I have a bouncing baby boy now, Gerald Jr. We call him GJ. And, the church has moved into a bigger building. You'll have to come visit. It's really hard being the first lady and a new Mom, but it's a blessing girl. Well call me sometimes. I'll be praying for you and you do the same for me.* I thought, "And if my prayer is answered, you'll never call me again." At one time I thought Carla was a friend, but after I broke up with Gerald I found out some things about Carla that proved otherwise. Like, she knew all along that Gerald and I were seeing each other and purposely set out to undermine our relationship. But, like I said before, she would hate the thought of me living out her dream of being a Pastor's wife. Poor Carla. Gerald has a lust problem. She's going to need all the prayer she can get to keep that husband of hers faithful.

    I thought the 3rd call was Terry. Not! Boy was I surprised to hear from Derek Dunn. I have got to get my number changed. *Well, well, Miss Mia. Bet you never thought you'd hear from me again. I know you've probably been wondering about me so, wonder no more, baby. A brotha has been living pret-TY large these days. Yes, Virginia has been good to me! You have no idea what you missed out on. If you're ever in town, look me up if you can find me. You might just see me cruising in my Mercedes sl500. But you can't come to my 3 story 5000 square foot house, though, 'cause you're not invited! Ha ha ha, talk about THAT at the water cooler! Oh and remember when I said you're a Queen? I lied. You ain't shit. You ain't about....* I hit the skip button. Back in the day, I would have *69'd him to give him a piece of my mind. Instead, I laughed hysterically. Derek was so unstable. I saved the message though. Just in case I ever need a good laugh, that message will work perfectly.

I called Black Diamonds and told Felecia I wouldn't be coming in Saturday morning. I'm kinda anal about my hair. I don't like too many hands in it…been there—done that—didn't work. Besides, Terry is the only one who knows exactly how I like it. Plus, Felecia use to date Eric Banks a few years ago. People say that's how he financed his club, The Diaspora. Apparently he used Felecia for her good credit. A baby and a bankruptcy later, he dumped her and left her struggling. I liked Felecia. She always smiled. Even though she never said anything, she looked real hurt when she overheard me telling Terry about my date with Eric. She was too pretty to be pining away over a loser like Eric. Had I known about their history before I met him I never would have given him the time of day. All I really wanted was to wait by the phone for Terry's call. Imagine that…Mia Gentry waiting by the phone for a man to call her. But this wasn't just any man. This was *my* man. Yes. I am finally staking claim. Poor, poor pitiful Stephanie; she was going to pretend to be so heartbroken. I said, *pretend.* I still was not convinced that she was as into Terry as she claimed. She was kidding herself if she thought for one minute that she'd have a future with Terry. Ha! We'll just see who POPs out of whose SPACE!

On Saturday I waited around until 1:30 for my man to call. Finally, I couldn't wait anymore. I had to run to Walgreen's to get some Midol. The cramps were kicking my butt. They had me knotted up like the naps on the back of Don King's head. That run took me all of 20 minutes and wouldn't you know it, that's when Terry called. *Hey Mia. I'm still in New York. I'm coming home on Wednesday instead of Tuesday though. I ordered something and it won't be ready until Tuesday evening, so it works out better if I leave Wednesday morning. Anyway, I've made some major decisions about some things and I can't wait to share them with you. I especially can't wait to see the look on your face when you see what I designed. I think you will be pleased...and very surprised. Meet me at Palomino's Wednesday at 6. I've already made reservations. Can't wait to see you. Love ya. Peace.*

    Okay. Now, let's dissect the message. He's in New York. What could he be doing in New York? He never said this was a business trip, so it could be personal. But I now know Stephanie's not with him, because when I called Black Diamonds to cancel, Felecia teased that "ya'll heifers must think Terry's the only person on earth who can do hair" because Stephanie and two of his other regulars had just called to cancel too. Wait a minute...I think there is a Tiffany's in New York...umm...I could be wrong. Maybe it's Jacob the Jeweler. No, I think its Tiffany's. He ordered something...what if it's a ring? He did say he designed whatever it is...what else do people design besides clothes and buildings. Clothes and buildings...nope that ain't it. It's a ring. He's made some decisions...he can't wait to share them with me...can't wait to see the look on my face...and he wants me to meet him at Palomino's. Well, that's definitely a few steps up from Johnny Carino's. I mean,

Palomino's is cozy, secluded, very private…just the kind of place you would take someone to for a romantic evening. What could be more romantic than …say…a proposal? Terry never ends a conversation with, "Love Ya". It's either, Peace, Peace Out, Peace in the middle east...Peace to the motherland, but never Love ya, Peace. He said, Love ya. Ok. Stop it, Mia! Don't get ahead of yourself…just slow your roll! Breathe. Breathe.

I took off work Monday, Tuesday and Wednesday just to prepare for Wednesday evening. I went to the spa and got a full body massage, a seaweed wrap, a mud bath, a facial, manicure, pedicure, arched eyebrows, legs waxed and I had my teeth whitened. (Not that they needed to be) I also changed my mind and let Felecia do my hair. I was so nervous on Wednesday. I was feeling things I've never felt before. I had never been in love before. So, this is what it feels like. Mmm.

I got to Palomino's at exactly 5:50. I wanted to make an entrance so I could see Terry light up when I arrived. So, the plan was to wait in the ladies lounge, check myself out again, and pull myself together. Then I would wait until 6:04 – 05 and make my entrance. Terry was on time for everything so I knew this plan would work. And, it did. I must say, I looked really nice in my silk A-line Kimono dress from Macy's. No name brands: that night I wanted Terry to see what I have inside of me, not what I was so use to perpetrating on the outside.

"Hey you!"

Terry stood up and gave me a big bear hug. "Hey Mia."

His smile said it all. He was glad to see me. "Before you say anything, I'm not late. I just had to stop in the ladies lounge for a minute to check myself out." I giggled. I hoped it wasn't too obvious that I was extremely excited.

"You look wonderful." Terry's eyes were roving my body, head to toe.

We laughed, talked and reminisced about old times throughout dinner and dessert. But by the time coffee came the laughing had stopped and Terry began to talk serious. This is it I thought. Here it comes.

"Mia."

"Yes." I also wanted to say, "I will." Thank God I didn't. I didn't want to be overzealous before he even popped the question. I didn't want to steal his thunder. I wanted to hear everything he had to say to me, everything. So I sat there with a little smile on my little face.

"You know I told you there's something I want to talk to you about. But first, there are some things I need to say to you."

"Ok. I'm listening." I wanted him to know, this wouldn't be like the last time he tried to talk to me.

"Here lately I've been going through some things and I've been thinking about where I'd like to see myself in a couple of years. I've accomplished a lot that I'm proud of, but I hadn't had anyone to really share those things with. I'm tired of living the single life, Mia. The whole dating scene is…it's a game I don't want to play anymore. I'm ready to settle down, get married, and be a father. I want to be able to enjoy all that I've worked for with a family: my own family. It's hard for a man in my position to find a woman who loves me for me. Someone who loves me unconditionally and not for the material things or the lifestyle I can afford." He took a deep breath and hesitated for a minute. I was thinking, *Come on Terry, come on, you can do it. You're my little engine that could. Yes you are...* "But I found her. It's funny how I was looking for something when suddenly I realized what I wanted in a soul mate was standing right in front of me. And to think, I almost let her get away." I had been thinking the same thing!, another sign that we belonged together. Great minds think alike! Terry grabbed my hand. I so conveniently had it lying in the middle of the table and not just so he could see my fresh manicure. Very slick Mia, very slick. I rubbed his hand with my thumb hoping he could hear the voice inside of me saying, "Yes I will, I do…YES!"

Then he said, "I have something to show you." When he let go of my hand I repositioned myself to sit up real proper and leaned in a bit. That way he wouldn't be too far away from me when we kissed. Terry pulled out a small purple velvet pouch. He knows purple is one of my favorite colors. "This is what I designed and ordered from Tiffany's while I was in New York." Ha! I was right! I was right!

"Oh. What is it?" I asked ever so cluelessly …as if I didn't know.

Terry pulled out the most gorgeous flawless oval 3-carat ring with a roll of baguettes on each side mounted in platinum. My radar kicked in and clocked that baby at at least $50 g's. All I could do was gasp. All of the preparing I did for this moment went out the window, and I struggled to find some words.

"Terry. Oh, my God! It's beautiful!" I felt my eyes begin to well up.

"Yeah? So, you think I did good?"

"Yeah," I said. "You did real good. I love it." I was just about to hold out my hand when Terry said…

"Great, because if you love it, then I know Stephanie will too. You two have the same taste in jewelry."

My face was cracked like Humpty Dumpty's ass. It took everything I had within me to keep that smile on my face and hold back my tears, but I managed to say, "You're right. We do. She's going to love it." I was in such a fog I couldn't hear whatever else Terry was saying. His voice was fading in and out as though I was about to lose consciousness. I pretended to check my watch. I said, "Wow, I didn't realize it was getting so late. I have to go." I opened my purse and pulled out MY half of the meal.

"Mia, No…I got this."

"Oh, no Terry. Don't be ridiculous. I didn't really expect for you to choose me, uh, treat me." I pulled my own chair out, stood up, dusted myself off and said, "Congratulations. I'm real happy for you, you and Stephanie." I managed to maintain my composure until I got to the restaurant's garage. Then I ran. I jumped in my car, hid behind my tinted windows and cried like a baby, just like I did when Luther died. On the way home the radio station played Anyone Who Had a Heart, then A House is Not a Home back-to-back. Was the DJ trying to KILL ME? Was I not suffering enough?!? Why? Why? Why?

The next couple of weeks were rough. I was hurting from my head to my toes—literally and figuratively. The only time I left my house was to go to Piccomolo's for a triple scoop of Cookies and Cappuccino Italian ice cream…four times. I called in sick to work, I missed an appointment with Ling Dau to get my hands and feet done, and I definitely didn't go to Black Diamonds. Terry left four messages on my answering machine, but I couldn't bear to respond. Someone had come over four times but I couldn't even answer the door. I even had four zits on my forehead from all the stress. The number four seemed to be a recurring motif in my life. Maybe because I was a forlorned woman destined to be forgotten and alone forever, while Stephanie Foreman stole all my good fortune. Forget that!

I got up and looked in the mirror. The reflection was painful, but underneath the extremely bad bed-head, and the red eyes underlined with bags packed for heartbreak hotel, was the old Mia Gentry, the confident woman who made the men all pause when she walked into a room; the vibrant Mia whose girlfriends and coworkers (some of them anyway) found her a joy to be around (I think). At that moment I decided I would cry no more tears for Terry Richmond. It was HIS loss! "Girl, first you need some rest to get rid of the bags. Then you need another day at the spa." It was only four o'clock in the afternoon—figures—but I went to bed and got some much needed sleep.

I woke up the next morning feeling refreshed. I even had a new perspective about my whole situation. I had gone from being sad to mad about Terry's plans, but now I felt almost happy for him. If Stephanie is who makes him happy, then that's who he should be with—even if I believe I could make him happier. It wasn't about me. Hmm. It wasn't about me. That's the first time I'd ever felt that way. I must really love Terry, because I want his happiness even more than I want my own.

I got the works at the spa, the six-hour Day of Dreams treatment. It included a relaxing body massage, deep-cleansing spa facial, spa manicure and pedicure, haircut and style (yes, I let them do my hair—they weren't Terry, but I was pleased with the results), make-up application, and a decadent lunch with a glass of expensive Tuscany wine. Afterwards, I went home and put on my Emilio Pucci pink printed dress (yes, I know this one's even too expensive for me; but I treated myself to it one day after a much deserved raise). Once I was looking drop dead gorgeous, I headed over to Terry's house. When I pulled in front of the house, I saw Stephanie's car in the driveway. Perfect. I wanted them both to be there. Stephanie answered the door.

"Mia? What are you doing here?"

"Well, hello to you too, Stephanie." I gave her a genuine smile. I hadn't realized how pretty Stephanie was. She was wearing some faded jeans and a casual t-shirt. Her shoulder length hair was pulled back in a ponytail. She looked like the perfect housewife. Maybe she is the best woman for Terry.

"I'm sorry. We just weren't expecting you." She looked concerned. "Come on in. Terry." Terry came from another room, and I swear his face lit up when he saw me. Don't go there, Mia. It's back to friends only. It was never anything else to Terry, so he's just happy to see his dear friend.

"Hey stranger!" He gave me a big bear hug. I could see Stephanie from the corner of my eye, and she didn't look too happy, so I patted Terry on the back and pulled away. "Where have you been? You didn't return my calls. I even came by your house once." Stephanie gave him a "you did what?" glare on that one. "I would have called the police, but when I saw Crystal for her appointment Tuesday, she said she had talked to you."

Crystal talked so much that sometimes she didn't even know what she was saying. I hadn't talked to her in months. "I had some vacation time to use, so I decided to take a couple of weeks off for some me time. I didn't mean to worry you." Terry and I were looking at each other like long lost lovers. What was that all about? He wants me. He wants me, bad. No. No. Mia, you're imagining it. Whatever I was imagining was snatched out of my head when Stephanie threw her hand up in my face.

"BAM! Look Mia! Have you heard the news?" She waved my, I mean her engagement ring in the air and got all antsy like she had to use the bathroom.

"It looks even more beautiful on you then it did in Terry's hand. Congratulations."

"You've seen it?" Uh-oh. Stephanie had a "no you didn't" look on her face. She looked from me to Terry, then back to me.

"Uh, yeah. Terry was so excited about the proposal that I guess he had to tell somebody. No big deal." Awkward silence....

"So, to what do we owe the pleasure of your visit?" It didn't sound like she really thought it was a pleasure to see me, but she did force a smile.

"Oh." I smiled back and handed her a gift bag from Saxs Fifth Avenue. "I wanted to be the first to congratulate the two of you on your engagement."

"What if I hadn't already proposed?" Terry nudged me on my arm and grinned.

"Well, you sounded like it was going to happen soon. Plus, I didn't know that Stephanie would be here, so I was planning just to leave it with you," Another awkward gaze between Terry and I.

"Well, then, it was a good thing that I am here and that my wonderful fiancé has already asked for my hand in marriage." Stephanie wrapped her arms around Terry's waist and laid her head on his shoulder.

"Yes. What luck. Anyway, that's all I stopped by for. I'll get out of you love birds' hair."

"Let me walk you out, Mia." Stephanie reluctantly let go of "her fiancé" so that he could walk out with me. We walked silently to my car. I reached for the door to open it, but Terry stopped me.

"Mia, I don't buy the vacation bit. What's been going on? I share with you my life-changing plan to propose to Stephanie, and you almost run out of the restaurant, then I don't hear from you for two weeks. What's up?"

It's now or never, Mia. Tell him, but don't tell him. Let him know how much you care so that you don't have any "what if" regrets later. Give him just enough information to make him think. "Okay, you're right." I looked towards the house and saw Stephanie peeking out of a window. "We've been friends for a long time, but over the past few months, it turned into something more for me. I care a lot about you and I had some crazy thoughts about us. It upset me a little when you told me about your proposal, and I needed some time to regroup, that's all." Terry looked shocked.

"Mia. I…uh."

"You don't have to say anything. I'm over it. I was lonely and I read some print that wasn't in the book, that's all. Really, I…I'm really happy for you and Stephanie. I think you'll have a great life together. And, I wish you nothing but happiness. You deserve it."

Terry's expression went from shock to the look he gives me when I've said something stupid and pissed him off. "You were lonely and you're over it, huh?" He shook his head. "You're right. Stephanie and I will have a great life together." Terry opened my car door with a little jerk.

"Terry—I didn't mean—well, you know…"

"Don't worry about it Mia. You're happy for Stephanie and me; I'm happy for you and yourself. You always work best that way. Nobody can love you as much as you love yourself."

Where was this coming from? He was upset. "What the hell was that for? That was a mean thing to say."

"Whatever, Mia. I don't have time for this."

"Time for what? What did I do this time?"

"Nothing."

I didn't know what to say, and I was mad. How dare he? Why would he say something like that to me? I got in my car and slammed the door. Then on my way home it hit me. Maybe Terry really did want me. He was upset because I told him how I felt and then dismissed it like it had just been a passing fancy. Maybe Terry had wanted me all this time, but just thought I didn't want him. Maybe Stephanie was his second choice. But why was that my fault? No, I hadn't told him how I felt before, but he never told me how he felt either. I pulled over into a grocery store parking lot and grabbed my cell phone. Terry picked up on the third ring.

"Terry, it's me. I've got to know what just happened. Are you mad at me?"

Silence, then, "No. I'm sorry. That was unfair. A lot of things have gone unsaid between us that should have been said a long time ago. But it doesn't matter now."

"How could it not matter, Terry? Please tell me whatever it is you need to say."

"No. You're a great friend, and I'll never have another friend like you. By the way, your hair looked great. And you owe me $140 for your two missed appointments."

I couldn't believe that Terry had reduced our relationship to $140. "Move on, Mia." That's what I told myself, and that's exactly what I planned to do. The first step was to find another new church home, and new gym, and a new beautician. This was getting ridiculous. From now on I wasn't getting involved with anyone who frequented any of my places of refuge. That sounds familiar. Have I said that before? Anyway, I mean it this time.

❦❧❦

I started to spend a lot of quality time with myself, and this time it wasn't code for "Me and my man split and I don't have anybody else right now." I picked up a new Walter Mosley murder mystery from the bookstore and spent my lunchtime reading in the park. After a couple of weeks it became a mental and physical break that I looked forward to. I hadn't forgotten about Terry, but I also hadn't been remembering him every second of the day. Hmm. I guess that old saying is true: time does heal all wounds. Unfortunately, the bigger the wound, the longer it takes to heal. But I found just the band-aid that I needed one afternoon in the park.

"Excuse me, Miss. Do you mind sharing this bench?"

"I glanced up at the 3 other benches nearby. One of which was completely vacant. I didn't even look at the stranger when I said, "The lighting is just as good over there," and waved my hand in the direction of the empty bench.

"Yes, but I like this light."

Okay, that was annoying. Couldn't he take a hint? With my nose still in my book, I said, "Whatever." Then I mumbled, "Even though I've been sitting here by myself, minding my own business, every day for the past two weeks, and right at this time. Go ahead, I don't own the park and my name is not on the bench."

"Okay. And if it did have your name on it, would it read Eva, as in deliver us from…?"

That's when I looked up at him. Nice, real nice. I smiled and we both laughed a little. I was looking at his face, but I wanted to give him the once over. It would be too obvious from this angle so I gestured for him to sit down and pretended to glance down shyly with embarrassment, but I was really checking him out. "I'm sorry. It's been a long day, and it's only noon." I sat my book in my lap, "Miarian. My name is Miarian." I don't know why I gave him my given name. He just seemed very smooth and classy, and Miarian seems much more sophisticated than Mia. "And you are?"

"D. Victor King." He held out his hand and I extended mine.

"So what is the D for? Or did you say THE Victor King, like you're some kind of celebrity or something?" He smiled.

"The D stands for Dashiell. I'm not a celebrity. Besides, you're the one sitting here looking like a movie star, unwilling to let us ordinary folk bask in your glow." Then I smiled. "My friends call me Vic. You can call me Vic."

"Well, Vic, my friends call me Mia." I exchanged phone numbers with Vic and I'm glad I did. Over the following week we met a few times for lunch, dinner and a movie. He was just what I needed to take my mind off Terry. Sometimes we would even take long walks in the park during lunch for the sole purpose of getting to know each other, no perpetrating, no pretense, just two people enjoying each other's company. That was really relaxing. I found myself becoming quite fond of Vic. He was easy and uncomplicated. I liked that.

It was 11:30 Friday night when the phone rang. Surprisingly, I was still up. "Hello?"

"Hey Mia, it's Crystal. I'm sorry to call you so late but I really need a favor."

"Oh, no. I'm not interested in dating another one of your psycho cousins...no, the answer is no!" I was as serious as a heart attack but for some reason Crystal got a big kick out of that.

"Girl no, that's not it. Seriously though, the exterminator came and sprayed my apartment building earlier today and the smell of that pesticide is making me ill. Do you mind if I come crash at your place tonight?"

"Ok, now that, I can help you with. Come on over."

Crystal was a good friend. She did have a big mouth and, like I said before, telephone, telegraph, teleCrystal; and knowing that is the reason I hesitated to confide in her about Vic. Crystal is a regular at Black Diamonds and I really didn't want my business in the shop. I didn't want Terry to think that I was sending him a message that I had moved on. Yeah. I still cared what Terry thought about me. I even hoped that one day we could get past all the drama and rekindle our friendship. I'm sure Stephanie would try to block that as well. She's such a player hater.

Crystal came over with a bottle of cheap wine to thank me for letting her stay. After 3 glasses I was singing like a canary. This is what I told her: "You know Crystal, sometimes when you least expect it, you meet your soul mate. Someone you can laugh with, cry with and tell anything, knowing that he won't hold it against you. Vic is so wonderful. He's everything I want in a man."

"Mia, uh, everything like what? 'Cause, uh, this is like déjà vu. I know I've heard you say that before."

"Yeah but this is different. I mean…he's got it all together. He's an anesthesiologist. He only works 9 months out of the year and that's because he makes so much money that if he didn't, he'd have to pay back too much in taxes. So during his 3 months off, he volunteers at a Christian facility that houses emotionally disturbed and troubled youths. He gives them bible based counseling, and he is so humble about it. He's great?"

"Yeah, sure Mia." Crystal pretended to be half-listening or maybe she was half-drunk, but I knew that sista was taking it all in. She is so transparent.

"You'll have to meet him, Crystal. He runs in marathons once a year and remember, you were talking about training for one? Maybe he can give you some pointers."

Saturday, a few hours after Crystal left, since I wasn't going to Black Diamonds I decided to go shopping. I had been watching this Juicy Couture Betsy Suede Hobo bag at Neiman Marcus, hoping I'd catch it on sale. It was! It was marked down 20% from $350.00 to $280.00. This was already a good day! I stopped at Music Warehouse before I left the mall. I was trying to find the latest Najee cd for Vic. We had gotten into the habit of surprising each other with little sweet nothing gifts, just to say, "I'm thinking of you." That's when I heard a familiar voice on the other side of the display. It was that old sickening, whining, syrupy voice that could only belong to Stephanie. Oh, my God, I thought. There goes my good day. Stephanie sounded like she was in a bad mood. Hmm, may be a good day after all.

"'Here and Now', 'You and I', what difference does it make? Just get something."

"Ms Foreman, please calm down. I know this is stressful but you're getting a case of the pre-wedding jitters. I totally understand. I'm your wedding planner. Let me do my job and you go over to Victoria's Secret and find yourself something real nice for the honeymoon. I will meet you in front of Chanel and we'll pick up that nice perfume you like to wear."

"No. Meet me at the Zodiac Room in Neiman Marcus. I need a drink."

Shoot! Just as I tried to escape the path of Bridezilla she roared my name.

"Mia?"

I turned around slowly to give my face time to hide my thoughts. "Ummm…" I pretended to forget her name. I thought that was a nice touch. I was getting over Terry but I still wasn't a fan of Stephanie. But, it's a new day. "…Stephanie. How are you?"

"Fine. Great. Never better. Getting married soon."

"Right, right. I guess my invitation got lost in the mail. But that's cool. I have plans for that day anyway."

"But you don't even know what day it is."

"Whatever day it is, I have plans."

"Oh, yeah, with your new beau…what's his name…Vic, right?"

She sounded like she didn't really believe I had a man. No she didn't! But wait a minute. How did she know about Vic anyway?

Wow! I knew Crystal was good but I didn't know she was that good. I just told her about Vic the night before and already she's broadcasting the news. She's better than CNN. "As a matter of fact, that's right." I was smug but Stephanie's demeanor changed. Uh-oh. She looked like she had something else to say again. I remember that look.

"Mia. Let's be straight with each other, woman to woman. Even if you are seeing someone else, it's hard for me to believe that you don't still have feelings for Terry. Do you? Are you still in love with my fiancé?"

"I've never told you that I was ever in love with Terry. Besides, what difference does it make now, Stephanie? You're getting married soon. You win. You're the one he chose."

"That's the problem, Mia. You always thought this was a game."

"Grow up Stephanie. Life's a game. However, I quit this one a long time ago."

"Yeah, but your pawn is still on the board."

"Whatever that means. Have a nice life, Stephanie. I gotta go." I turned to walk out, and was half way to the door when Stephanie rushed up and grabbed my arm.

"Mia, wait. I have to make this right."

༺❀༻

Stephanie and I talked for quite a while. We both put our egos in check and for the first time talked to each other openly and honestly. All the way home I couldn't stop thinking about what she said to me. The whole conversation made me look at her in a different light. She wasn't the phony, gold-digger I made her out to be at all. Instead, she was a woman with feelings, wants, desires and insecurities just like me. Only she was in tune with all of her drama, and she held back nothing. She knew her self-worth. I envied her. I never in a million years would have imagined that she would be the one I would take council from. We learned a lot about each other from that conversation. We weren't instantly best buds but this was a start. It was nice to know that we had more in common than just Terry. Before I walked away I hugged Stephanie and she hugged me back. We both agreed that ultimately it was Terry's happiness that we both wanted now, henceforth and forevermore.

※

The day of the wedding was a perfect fall day. A gentle breeze blew through the air, strewing orange, gold, brown, and yellow leaves all over the church lawn. There was a slight overcast, but the sun shone through just enough to dance off the small duck pond that decorated the west side of the building. As I opened the outside doors to the church, the wonderful aroma of jasmine came pouring out and almost made me dizzy, you know, the kind of dizzy you get when you're so relaxed and peaceful that you could just float on air. When I walked in, the foyer was empty. I sneaked a peak through the small window on the sanctuary door. The place was absolutely gorgeous! White chiffon scarves cascaded down each aisle, connected to each pew with an assortment of orange and peach roses, yellow lilies, bright daffodils, and sun-drenched chrysanthemums. The bridesmaids were beautiful in their full-length sand matte satin gowns. The groomsmen were too fine in their tuxes with retro-ivory, paisley pattern, five button vests. Clean! There were more people here today than I had ever seen on a Sunday morning! I saw mutual friends of Terry, Stephanie and mine, and lots of Black Diamond patrons. Wow! Even Terry's mother showed up. It was good to see her sitting on the front row and in rare form. That was a good thing. Those two big Charles Dutton looking brothers were sitting next to her, though. But that was also a good thing.

I could see Stephanie's side profile. She looked so beautiful. The baby's breath in her hair almost made it look like she had a halo. Any man would be blessed to have her for a wife. And then there was my friend, my best friend, Terry, standing at the altar. Now that was a sight to behold. He looked like…he looked like himself. There was no need to compare him to Denzel, Shamar, Taye Diggs, or Morris Chestnut. Shoot, he looked better than all of them. Terry was in a class all by himself. I'd never seen him so happy. I swear I saw a tear roll down his cheek.

The usher caught my eye and let me know it was okay for me to walk in. When the door opened there were peach rose petals covering the white carpet leading to the altar. Gerald Albright's instrumental version of Luther Vandross's 'So Amazing' began to play. It was truly amazing. My Dad grabbed my arm, kissed my cheek, and led me down the aisle to my future as Mrs. Terry Richmond.

"I do."

"I do."

As Terry and I were leaving the church, I tried to look upon as many of the faces of those who helped me, knowingly and unknowingly, become the woman I am today. I saw Pastor Morgan and Carla. They actually looked happy, and the baby was beautiful. Unfortunately, just as I started to look away, I saw the Pastor look me up and down, and lick his lips. Lord, help him. I saw Vincent Cartwright. Now, who wears a muscle shirt to a wedding?! Dr. Damon O'Neill was there with a lovely young lady. Is she wearing nurse's shoes? And is that one of Terry's momma's "helpers" sitting on the other side of him? There's Eric Banks. I'm gonna' be sure to look later to see if he brought a gift. Derek was sitting with a large group of people from my job. He was actually scowling at me! Then there was Dashiell Victor King. What an awesome man. He graciously bowed out when I told him about Terry. He said he always knew that something was holding me back, and that he just wanted me to be happy.

"Your chariot awaits you, my queen." Terry's smile made me weak in the knees. I looked back over my shoulder before climbing in the Rolls Royce, and I think I saw Stephanie trying to put the moves on Vic! Love couldn't happen to two better people (oh, I mean besides Terry and me). Stephanie and I made eye contact and she read my lips say, "Thank You." She gave me a wink and returned her attention to Vic. Do your thang, girl.

I will never forget how I felt at that very moment. For the first time in my life, in all honesty, I could say that I was truly happy. I started out looking for a man fit to the fifth and in the process I became a woman fit to have that kind of man. God works in mysterious ways. He's still working on me, though. I'm not perfect—but I am fit; spiritually, physically, emotionally, financially, and mentally. Mia Gentry grew up. Oops! I mean Mia Richmond.

"I love you, husband."

"I love you too, wife. And I have something I can't wait to show you."

"Oooooooooooooooooo Terry!"

www.ingramcontent.com/pod-product-compliance
Lightning Source LLC
Chambersburg PA
CBHW031405040426
42444CB00005B/422